GOURMET FOOD
ON A
WHEAT-FREE DIET

GOURMET FOOD
ON A
WHEAT-FREE DIET

Fourth Printing

By

MARION N. WOOD

Globe, Arizona

With a Foreword by

WILLIAM E. BISHOP, M.D.

CHARLES C THOMAS · PUBLISHER
Springfield · Illinois · U.S.A.

Published and Distributed Throughout the World by

CHARLES C THOMAS ● PUBLISHER

Bannerstone House

301-327 East Lawrence Avenue, Springfield, Illinois, U.S.A.

© *1967, by* CHARLES C THOMAS ● PUBLISHER

ISBN 0-398-02117-1

Library of Congress Catalog Card Number: 66-24651

First Printing, 1967
Second Printing, 1972
Third Printing, 1975
Fourth Printing, 1979

With **THOMAS BOOKS** *careful attention is given to all details of manufacturing and design. It is the Publisher's desire to present books that are satisfactory as to their physical qualities and artistic possibilities and appropriate for their particular use.* **THOMAS BOOKS** *will be true to those laws of quality that assure a good name and good will.*

Printed in the United States of America

R-1

TO MY HUSBAND, MIKE

To my husband, Mike
whose recovery made this research worthwhile
and
to his doctor, William E. Bishop, M.D.
who saved his life

FOREWORD

The health of modern man has been greatly influenced and improved with the advent of antibiotics and chemical agents to control his infections; purified natural and synthetic hormones to replace what the body is lacking; pharmacological agents to aid his disturbed mental processes; potent chemical agents and radiation agents to treat his malignant diseases; electronic and mechanical devices to correct or temporarily take over the function of his heart, lungs, or kidneys, and highly skilled surgical procedures to correct congenital defects and removed diseased tissue.

However, amidst all of these advances in medicine, there is still one other avenue which he may follow for the improvement of his health—this is the adjustment of his diet to the demands and idiosyncrasies of his body metabolism.

Even in Hippocratic times, it was noted that people were benefited by the addition or deletion of some foodstuffs from their daily diet. Today every woman's magazine and every Sunday supplement of the newspaper contains diet plans—some of which are based primarily upon food fadism and others of which are well founded upon the needs and demands of the patient's disturbed physiology. Certainly the low salt diet, the low cholestrol diets, the special diets for the diabetic, the restricted diets for the allergic people, and the low calorie diet for the unhappy obese individual are fairly commonplace.

There is, however, a group of individuals who have what is called "malabsorption syndrome." The presence of certain food substances in the diet may so affect the intestinal tract that it is unable to absorb nutritional elements into the blood stream. As a result of this, the patient experiences a gradual physical deterioration, due not only to the immediate effect upon the intestinal tract, but also due to the marked disturbances which can occur in the various chemical constituents of the blood. These disturbances may in turn produce secondary changes in the function of the heart, kidneys, and liver.

One of the more particular forms of malabsorption began to receive attention in 1949 when it was demonstrated by some physicians in the Netherlands that certain infants who received wheat in their diet experienced a gradual deterioration in their health because of the development of vomiting, abdominal pain, diarrhea, and loss of appetite. Careful analysis of food substances indicated that gluten, the water insoluble wheat protein, was the "poison" which made the children sick.

Those individuals unable to properly utilize gluten are stated to be suffering from "gluten-enteropathy." This particular terminology separates these individuals from other patients who may experience malabsorption problems which may be caused by entirely different metabolic disturbances. Persons suffering from gluten-enteropathy must diligently control their diet, for many of them are highly sensitive to the minutest amount of gluten in their food, and a small amount of this material may produce a recurrence.

Many of our food products on the market will contain gluten despite the fact that information on the package would seem to indicate there is no wheat or allied grain material in the product.

This present volume, *Gourmet Food On A Wheat-Free Diet,* is the outgrowth of much painstaking effort by the wife of one of my patients who was found to be highly sensitive to gluten. The book is presented not as a collection of standard recipes and instructions from a research diet kitchen to tell the patient what he should eat and not eat, but it is the by-product of the individual effort of a housewife who was charged with the task of providing a nutritious diet for her ailing husband. The person who is entrusted with the chore of cooking and planning meals for the patient who needs an absolutely gluten-free diet often encounters dismal failures in the preparation of a palatable meal three times a day, seven days a week, 365 days a year, year in and year out. Standard diets and recipes which are obtainable from many sources often fail to reveal the pitfalls one may encounter in buying foodstuffs and subsequently in preparing them. When the writer was first instructed to put her husband on a wheat-free diet, the diet consisted of a few standard recipes which were given her. She soon found that these were not completely adequate to supply variety and nutrition in the daily preparation of meals. She has spent a great many hours in trial and error with various food products, many of which unsuspectingly contained gluten. Her six years' experience in the average home kitchen has led to the accumulation of a great number of very palatable and nutritious recipes, and these she would share with other individuals who must prepare the meals for the patient who needs a gluten-free diet.

Although this program of cooking and feeding was developed for an individual who suffers from gluten-enteropathy it would be equally applicable to those patients who may manifest allergic disorders as the result of excessive ingestion of wheat.

These recipes are not presented as a form of food fadism or some transient enthusiasm for variation in eating habits, but they are presented for the benefit of those individuals whose physicians have definitely established the fact that they are unable to live a healthy life if their diet is contaminated with gluten.

I can attest to the palatability of the food prepared in accordance with these recipes, for I have often eaten in the writer's home; the effectiveness of the diet is manifest in the excellent state of health of her husband.

WILLIAM E. BISHOP, M.D.

Globe, Arizona

PREFACE

This cookbook is the culmination of six years of research and experimentation using rice flour as a basic flour and a substitution for wheat flour. At first I was concerned only with feeding my husband a nourishing, palatable diet. I was determined that meals would remain a pleasure—not an exercise in survival, which my earliest recipes and results seemed to forecast.

In retrospect, I believe that my life's experiences converged upon this challenging new problem. Teacher, social worker, and potter, my vocations and avocation, contributed to this book. I am sure that if I had never struggled with the empirical science of making glazes for my pottery I would never have dared to juggle recipes as much as I have—nor had the "hunches" that helped me so often.

My husband recognized the teacher in me, related to this problem, when that first year he gave me a valentine to "Dear Teacher." Now the social worker in me wants to share and help others beyond the small circle of my own known world, to help the segments of our population which the women's magazines with dietetic kitchens behind them have ignored.

ACKNOWLEDGMENTS

In the preparation of this cookbook, the author is indebted to many of her friends for recipes which she has used, either in the original form or adapted by her for cooking without wheat, rye, barley, or oats.

The author also wishes to express her gratitude to Barbara E. Gunning, Associate Professor, Division of Food and Nutrition, University of Arizona, for her wise counsel and for making herself available as a never-failing source of information and John V. Carbone, M.D., Associate Professor of Medicine, University of California, San Francisco Medical Center, for his time spent in reading the manuscript and for his encouragement.

The writer is very appreciative for the help given to her by Mrs. Mary K. Simmons, Gila County Home Economist, Agricultural Extension Service, University of Arizona.

M.N.W.

BEST RECIPE

Half a cup of friendship
And a cup of thoughtfulness,
Creamed together with a pinch
Of powdered tenderness,
Very lightly beaten
In a bowl of loyalty,
With a cup of faith and one of hope
And one of charity.
Be sure to add a spoonful each
Of gaiety-that-sings,
And also the ability
To laugh-at-little-things.
Moisten with the sudden tears
Of heart felt sympathy.
Bake in a good natured pan
And serve repeatedly.

—AUTHOR UNKNOWN

CONTENTS

Page

Foreword—William E. Bishop, M.D. .... *vii*
Preface—Marion N. Wood .... *xi*
Acknowledgments .... *xiii*
Best Recipe .... *xiv*

SECTION 1. Introduction 3
SECTION 2. Friends and Foes 8
SECTION 3. Bread—The Staff of Life 13
SECTION 4. Cakes, Fillings and Frostings 37
SECTION 5. Cookies, The Indispensable Sweet 49
SECTION 6. Desserts—Joy to the Sweet Tooth 60
SECTION 7. Pastry and Pies—Let's Be Special 75
SECTION 8. Main Dishes—Specialties of the House 84
SECTION 9. Having the "Last Word" 102
SECTION 10. Table of Comparison of Food Values of Wheat—
Rice—Soy 103

References 106
Glossary 107
Index 109

GOURMET FOOD
ON A
WHEAT-FREE DIET

Section 1

INTRODUCTION

In December, 1959, when our family physician told my husband that he should eliminate wheat, rye, barley, oats, and their derivatives from his diet, I doubt that even he dreamed that a "miracle" would take place before our eyes—almost a re-creation.

The new diagnosis was called nontropical sprue. The doctors also call it malabsorption syndrome, idiopathic steatorrhea, or, in children, celiac disease. Strangely, this fellow traveler of civilization was discovered during a famine in Holland in World War II. Dr. Dicke observed that children who had done favorably under starvation conditions began to fare less well with the re-introduction of cereals into their diet. The results of the research made by Dicke, Weijers, and van de Kamer were first reported in 1950. Later it was found that adults reacted in a like manner to removal of cereals from their diet. The detrimental factor found in wheat, rye, barley, and oats (but absent from corn, rice, soya, and potatoes) was shown to be present in gluten.

Wheat is Western Man's staff of life. In America, eating any meal usually means eating some portion of wheat or possibly barley, rye, or oats. For the housewife geared to our modern way of preparing food, the abrupt elimination of all gluten-bearing grains can be most disconcerting. She is completely dependent upon a cuisine intermingled with the use of wheat—far more than she would ever imagine.

Besides starch, wheat contains two proteins, gliaden and glutenin, which form gluten when liquid is added. This sticky substance in wheat is the reason for its good baking qualities. Every cook has had the annoyance of trying to

3

get the dough off the side of the dish, her hands, or the dish cloth if she has made bread. Gluten provides the elasticity of bread when baker's yeast or compressed yeast is added for leavening. When bread rises, the stretching of the elastic gluten holds in the bubbles of carbon dioxide which have been freed by the yeast. This makes a light and airy bread of fine texture. Although cake and pastry flour have less gluten, there is still sufficient left to cause the flour particles to stick together when liquid is added and the mass is stirred. When the cook rolls out a pie crust, she takes it for granted that she will be able to lift the sheet of dough onto her pie plate without its breaking or giving her too much trouble. There is elasticity to all wheat-flour dough or batter. However, if this same cook tries to use a flour which lacks gluten for her pie crust, using the same recipe, her dough breaks when lifted, breaks when she tries to lift even a small corner, and breaks into many pieces when she tries to fit it into a pie plate, completely thwarting the accomplishment of her goal. When she bakes this exasperating dough, she bites into a grainy, brittle substance which is far from pleasing to her tongue. In all of her cooking she will miss the job that gluten does, and her flours will not help her.

I was ill prepared for my new adventure in cooking, but the stakes were very high and I could learn. For twenty-three years my husband, Mike, had struggled to live. For twenty-three years fine dedicated doctors were baffled by his severe gastrointestinal upsets, and a good many of our hopes and plans, and all of our young years, marched together with this bafflement. In retrospect, we know that the bronchiectasis which was first diagnosed in 1941, and the allergies which he had had most, or all, of his life in some degree, had masked the basis for the gastrointestinal upsets. These had occurred widely-spaced at first, but later with increasing frequency. At times we clung desperately but fiercely to the faith that sometime the doctors would find the answer. Several of them went far beyond the call of duty in that attempt, but clinics, specialists, and general practitioners could not fit the puzzle together until that day in December, 1959, when our family physician found the missing clue.

Now I had an opportunity to help my husband return to health. I had one major task: to eliminate all irritating agents from his diet, but to make the food delicious and, I hoped, worthy of the standards set by my favorite general appeal magazines. I went to work on what was to be the most challenging, exciting, frustrating, and rewarding work of my life.

Mike was a very sick man that fall and winter of 1959, and his future, if there was to be a future, looked black. But within a week on his new diet he gained five pounds, in five weeks he gained twenty-five pounds, and in that first year he gained forty pounds, which brought him to the normal weight he has since maintained. Of course, the weight was of secondary importance. With the weight came health and vigor and a new life. In those early weeks and months, two factors worked together. First, the elimination of the gluten gliaden grains cleared the way for his new foods to nourish him. Second, the doctor supplemented his diet heavily with vitamins. There was no medication. Treatment was, and would continue to be, by food.

During this period of Mike's return to health and until his intestinal tract had calmed down, roughage foods (fruits, vegetables, and sometimes meats) were put through our blender, thus making their nourishing goodness available without irritation.

I vowed to continue to use the cook's creed, "I will prepare all meals to be as appealing to the eye and palate as I can. I will make every meal important." I started with four recipes using rice flour I found at a health food store (most of the regular markets carry only corn meal). These were the recipes that our doctor found. I could find none in

my cookbooks. Recipes using corn meal were also available, but the flavor of corn is too definite to use as a
steady diet. I was also seeking to approximate wheat flour
nutritionally if possible.

Later I found a book of allergy recipes. I soon found
that all of the special recipes I tried, and I tried many,
came out heavy, course-textured, often granular feeling on
the tongue, and generally screaming "diet." I wondered if
the ones who concocted the recipes actually ate the food.
It was very discouraging, especially since this type of
eating can kill one's enjoyment of all meals. Why was rice
flour used so little? Also, why could it not be used in a
regular manner as wheat is used? Some of the recipes
seemed very odd, but I had to learn why.

One cookbook stated that natural brown rice flour may
be used with skill, but failed to tell how to attain the skill!
I wrote to many possible sources for help, with most un-
satisfactory replies. Recipes were prepared for the masses
of people who eat wheat, I was told. That no one cared
about the weird diets was inferred.

Waffles, pancakes, muffins, and quick breads would be
used from now on in place of yeast breads. (Yeast bread
cannot be made without gluten as an ingredient.) By trying
and adjusting, re-trying and re-adjusting, delicious waffles
and pancakes were achieved. These were easiest to make
light and of pleasing texture as bread substitutes, and we
used them with increasing variations until I was quite
secure in my ability to produce good and uniform results.

With my courage fortified and my confidence mounting,
I launched into further experiments. These experiments
took me into a more difficult field—I now tried muffins,
bread, cookies, cakes, and pies. I learned that many of
my products were most successful when baked in small
sizes, that a muffin is usually better in texture than bread,
that I could make a better layer cake than a loaf cake, or
a better cupcake than a square tin cake. The old saying

that good things come in small packages is very true when cooking without gluten.

Finally, the questions which I set out to solve, "Why is rice flour used so little? and why could it not be used as a substitute for wheat flour? have been answered. By means of the adjustments which I show in this cookbook, rice flour can provide a very palatable diet. It is *rice,* not wheat of course, and does not taste *exactly* like wheat, but it can and does meet the standards I demand for taste, texture, lightness, and togetherness. Many of the products surpass the wheat products when put to the test. The constant requests which I receive for recipes attest to this. Actually, although I frequently eat products from the wheat world (since I am not a dieter), I find myself very critical of many of the foods (baked goods) prepared with wheat. They have texture, lightness, and togetherness, but too many now seem flat and tasteless.

Six years have passed. The former patient is full of energy and has maintained normal weight. He eats much less, but it nourishes him much more! He has never had an upset that we could not find the culprit by a little sleuthing. It is always the hidden part of a gluten-gliaden bearing grain. Because of consistent vigilance, he has probably not even averaged an upset a year, but the fact that it can and does happen emphasizes the doctor's original warning, "Once normal health has been restored, the gluten-free diet (rice, corn, soya, potato) must be continued indefinitely to avoid relapses.

But then, if one can eat gourmet food on a diet and the cook can see a dramatic recovery walk through her door each day, who cares?

Section 2

FRIENDS AND FOES

You will realize, no doubt, that even in foods all of us do not have the same friends. Happily, your circle may be wide. The diet which I have worked with is an "all-the-way" elimination of wheat, rye, barley, and oats. It is much easier to add to a diet than it is to substitute or subtract. Therefore, it is my hope that this section will be helpful to all who have a problem with grains—no matter the degree. In any case, your diet will be supplied by your doctor. This section merely points the way in looking for possible pitfalls.

My husband's doctor, as mentioned above, ordered a complete elimination of wheat, rye, barley, and oats. Experience has taught me that the derivatives or by-products of of these grains often spell "trouble." They are very, very sneaky since they are often found in unexpected places. In his six years experience on this diet, my husband has never been upset other than by a derivative or hidden part of the grain. Anything that can cause a three-day illness is important.

Malt and brewer's yeast are included as foes. Malt flavoring is used very widely and consequently excludes many foods that otherwise might be included. Following a couple of reactions by my dieter, who had partaken of root beer and a cream cheese dip, both of which we thought passed the elimination test, I did some research. Compton's Encyclopedia supplied this bit of information: "Barley or other grain that has been artificially germinated or sprouted by moisture is called malt—Yeast producers use malt as food for yeast plants." Compton's lists wheat as another grain used. Both the root beer and the cream cheese dip

8

contained brewer's yeast.

A cocktail made from a liquor which is distilled from a forbidden grain can be upsetting. Seasoning sauces are especially tricky as they may or may not include some of the offending grains. It is not enough to read the name of the product only, the ingredients which should be listed on the label *must always be checked*. Don't use any product which has omitted listing ingredients—such as many salad oil dressings, instant coffee that fails to state 100 per cent coffee, cocoa that does not list formula, or any prepared food.

Casually, one would assume that a diet using rice would mean that Chinese food would be free of pitfalls, but soy sauce is used very freely in many Chinese dishes. The sauce might or might not be wheat-free. Sometimes the label states only hydrolized protein. From what?

Mexican food is usually based upon the use of corn. Many of the dishes are wheat-free, but not all of them. A dish that is wheat-free in one restaurant may not be in the next. We were taken as guests to a very lovely Mexican restaurant with the anticipation that there would be no problem. When my dieter questioned the waiter about the inclusion of wheat flour in some of the recipes used, the waiter returned from the chef with the information that they used wheat flour in everything. This is unusual, however. In our area, he can eat tacos in one restaurant and in another they use gravy thickened with wheat flour to moisten the meat.

Soups are generally thickened with wheat flour; they often have barley present, and, rather frequently, brewer's yeast is also used. Consomme and bouillon, although clear and seemingly innocent of trouble (many think that they are just beef broth) are made from a conglomerate of many ingredients, several of which contain the enemy. The dieter must know what he is eating. Secret recipes are not for him.

Friend   *Foe*

Thickening Ingredients

Cornstarch

Potato flour

Rice flour or any of your flours

Arrowroot starch

Sago

Tapioca

Gelatin

Stick to your friends—the enemy can trip you here. Avoid all creamed or thickened foods when eating out. Unless you can *really know the thickening used.*

Desserts

Any made with your flour, such as pies, cakes, cookies, and puddings.

Gelatins and Jello

Homemade ice cream

Homemade sherbet

Junket

Tapioca

Fruit and dried fruits

The enemy has taken over in the commercial field. The supermarket is not for you—neither is the restaurant, for many desserts. You may find a few gelatin, jello, and cornstarch puddings available on the market shelves for you.

Beverages

Coffee (if labelled 100 per cent pure coffee)

Pure cocoa

Tea

Fruit juices

Carbonated beverages (perhaps)

Check instant coffee, also

Cocoa

Postum

Malted milk, Ovaltine

Root beer is considered a carbonated beverage. It can spell trouble.

Wine, Vermouth, Brandy

Rum

Most liqueurs

Tequila (made from the century plant south of the border)

Cognac

Gin, Whiskey, Vodka

Bourbon, probably

Watch that cocktail!

Beer or ale

Dairy Products

Milk

Eggs (plain)

Dairy products

A sneaky one too! Watch out for cream cheese dips. They may have a soup mix added,

Friend	*Foe*
Evaporated milk Condensed milk Cream All kinds of cheese	which in turn may have a foe present. Some cheese dips have brewer's yeast in them. Some have a sauce flavoring. Milk drinks such as malted milk, Ovaltine, and some cocoa drinks—Be Careful! Possibly an omelet may have some flour used in preparation. A fondue often does also. Foods dipped in egg usually have flour used also. Devilled eggs may have salad dressing containing flour used as an ingredient. Creamed eggs or egg croquettes may have the enemy present.
Cereals Cream of Rice Corn Meal Mush Hominy Rice Honey Rice Krinkles Puffed Rice	Many ready-to-eat cereals contain malt flavoring, *check your label.* Cornflakes contain malt flavoring.
Crackers and Substitutes Plain corn chips Potato chips (plain) This seems to be it unless you make your own.	Watch out for special seasonings on these. The barbecued ones, especially, may have a foe used as a seasoning. Commercial crackers in general.
Soups Your own homemade ones Chicken broth with nothing but salt added.	Bouillon, consomme, and all creamed soups. Bouillon and consomme are foes because grains are frequently used in mixture before it is strained into an unthickened liquid. *Read your labels.*
Meat, Fish and Poultry All very good friends when cooked plain	Cold cuts may have cereal used in them. *Check your label.*

Friend	*Foe*
	Canned meat dishes with gravy or sauce, commercial chili con carne, ravioli, croquettes—any product in this category *other than pure meat may mean trouble for you.* All breaded items. *All sauces unless you have checked the contents.* Any stuffing.
Miscellaneous (used in conjunction with main courses)	
Cider or apple vinegar	There is a question mark over distilled or malt vinegars. The National Institutes of Health in its booklet "Gluten-Free Diet," says "No," for soy sauce or Worcestershire sauce. This means they suspect the enemy to be present. *Be watchful.*
Meat tenderizer made from papaya; Adolph's is one brand.	Monosodium Glutamate is under a cloud. The authorities disagree.
Pure mayonnaise	
Oil dressings with approved contents.	Salad dressings
	Some oil dressings

READ EVERY LABEL ON EVERY PRODUCT. LEARN YOUR FOODS—AT LEAST TO THE EXTENT OF THE AREAS WHERE YOUR ENEMIES MAY BE FOUND.

Section 3

BREAD—THE STAFF OF LIFE

Your breads will all be "quick breads." Gluten, the sticky substance in wheat, is the reason for the flour's good baking qualities. Wheat flour, which is used as the basic flour for most bread, has over 90 per cent gluten content. The flours used in this cookbook for our dieters (namely rice, corn, soya, and potato flours) are lacking in gluten and have no togetherness. Gluten provides the elasticity of bread when baker's yeast is added for leavening. When the bread rises, the stretching of the elastic gluten holds in the bubbles of carbon dioxide freed by the yeast. This makes a light and airy bread of fine texture. You must compensate for the loss of this service. You must supply togetherness, lightness, and a fine texture. Your flour will not help you to do this since it is more like grains of extremely fine sand. In the absence of gluten, you will be unable to use baker's yeast. Your leavening will need to be increased considerably to accomplish your goal. Grittiness under the teeth is most unpleasant, but you will see how this can be overcome by using eggs, potato flour, and gelatin. The eggs are used for leavening and to supply togetherness; potato flour improves the texture of your baking when used in small qualities, and also serves as a binder; gelatin acts as a binder and provides moisture. Since your flour does not help you, the usual ratio of leavening to flour is abandoned for a much higher ratio. This throws you into a trial-and-error method or an empirical science, adjusting your tools to the goal which you seek. Good bread must be fairly light and airy, but it must slice well with a minimum of crumbs.

You can enjoy muffins, biscuits, popovers, waffles,

13

pancakes, coffee cake, or bread with as frequent a taste change as you are willing to stir. They all freeze happily so you can bake and store or mix and eat, just as you wish. You can also make your own mixes from the dry ingredients of these recipes. When we go on vacation I bake as much as I can efficiently plan to use, or perhaps I should say plan to use with relish. I pack the waffle iron and bake fresh waffles as desired. This is accomplished by using my dry mix in small quantities.

Most all of the breads made with gluten-free flours seem to be improved in taste and texture by the use of two or more flours. It is also obvious from studying the nutrient content tables that the resulting product is nutritionally improved. In this cookbook, natural brown-rice flour is used as the basic flour. Excepting for cookies, soya flour is usually used in a ratio of one-fourth soya to the entire flour content. Soya flour is naturally quite heavy.

> A loaf of bread, the Walrus said,
> Is what we chiefly need!

(Lewis Carroll—*Alice's Adventures in Wonderland.*)

Rice Sesame Seed Bread

A crusty, good-flavored bread which slices very well. I think of this as a basic bread for general use.

1 envelope plain gelatin	¾ teaspoon salt
¼ cup milk	3 teaspoons baking powder
1 cup milk	¼ cup sugar
2 cups brown rice flour	5 eggs
½ cup rice polish	2 tablespoons salad oil
2 tablespoons soya flour	½ cup toasted sesame seed
1 tablespoon potato flour	

Set oven at 350 degrees; place pan of water on bottom shelf. Line a pan 4½ x 8 inches and another 3¼ x 6 inches with wax paper folded double, and then grease. Soften gelatin in ¼ cup milk; place over low heat and melt gelatin, but don't boil it; set aside after adding the remaining cup of milk. Sift together all dry ingredients with the exception of the sesame seed; be sure that the flours are thoroughly blended. If not, sift again; add gelatin-milk mix, oil, and eggs; sprinkle the toasted sesame seed over the top and blend until thoroughly mixed. Pour into prepared pans, spread and flatten the batter into the corners. Bake larger tin for about one hour and the smaller for forty-five to fifty minutes.

Rice Sesame Seed Bread II

Lighter than the above bread, this does not slice quite as well. The flavor is much the same, just a little sweeter.

1 envelope plain gelatin	1 teaspoon salt
½ cup milk	2 tablespoons baking powder
1 cup milk	½ cup sugar or honey
2 cups brown rice flour	4 eggs
½ cup rice polish	½ cup salad oil
1 tablespoon potato flour	½ cup toasted sesame seed
2 tablespoons soya flour	

Set oven at 350 degrees; place small pan of water on bottom shelf. Line one pan 4½ x 8 inches and another 3¼ x 6 inches with wax paper folded double, and then grease. Soften gelatin in one-half cup milk; place over low heat and melt gelatin—do not boil; set aside after adding the remaining cup of milk. Sift together the flour, salt, baking powder, and sugar; add the eggs, oil, and gelatin-milk mixture; sprinkle the sesame seed over the top and blend until thoroughly mixed. Pour into prepared pans; spread and flatten the batter into the corners. Bake larger tin for one hour and the smaller for forty-five to fifty minutes.

Rice Bran Bread

This is a delicious bread which lends itself easily to taste variations.

Basic:

2 cups brown rice flour	4 egg yolks
½ cup soya flour	2 cups buttermilk
1½ cups rice bran	2 tablespoons salad oil
1 teaspoon salt	½ cup molasses, sugar,
1 tablespoon baking powder	or honey
1 teaspoon soda	½ cup raisins (optional)
2 tablespoons potato flour	4 stiffly beaten egg whites

Sift dry ingredients together. Add egg yolks, buttermilk, oil, and sweetening. Blend at low speed until well combined. Fold in stiffly beaten egg whites and raisins at the last. Bake in two pans 8 x 4½ inches for one hour at 350 degrees.

Variations:

Add the rind of one orange.

Use four teaspoons baking powder and omit soda. If you do this, use sweet milk.

Use one cup rice bran and substitute one-half cup rice polish for the remaining one-half cup rice bran.

Beat whole eggs until light and fluffy with the sugar, then add milk, and lastly fold in dry ingredients. This makes a little difference in the texture.

Orange-Date Bread

Good for tea sandwiches with cream cheese for filling.

2 cups brown rice flour	2 tablespoons potato flour
½ cup soya flour	4 eggs
½ cup rice polish	½ cup sugar
1 cup rice bran	Juice and rind of 1 orange,
1 teaspoon salt	fill cup with milk
1 tablespoon baking powder	1 more cup milk
1 teaspoon soda	2 tablespoons oil
½ cup finely chopped dates	

Sift flours, salt, baking powder, and soda together into bowl; add eggs, sugar, orange and milk, and oil; blend until well combined. Fold in dates. Bake in three tins 3¼ x 5¾ inches for forty-five to fifty minutes at 350 degrees.

Best Bread

I think that this bread comes closest to a bread for all uses of any that I make. The potato gives it a spongy texture which is very pleasing.

½ cup beaten mashed potato	3 teaspoons baking powder
¼ cup margarine or butter	1 teaspoon soda
¼ cup sugar	1 teaspoon Cream of Tartar
6 eggs, separated	½ teaspoon salt
1½ cups brown rice flour	⅛ teaspoon pepper (optional)
½ cup rice polish	¾ cup milk
2 tablespoons soya flour	

Be sure that the potato is lump free, measure one-half cup and cream it thoroughly with the margarine or butter and the sugar. Add the egg yolks one at a time, beating thoroughly after each addition. Sift the dry ingredients together and add to the potato-egg mixture alternately with the milk; fold in the egg whites which have been beaten to hold their shape in soft peaks—not stiff. Pour batter into tins and bake at 350 degrees for about one hour. This amount will make one loaf 9½ x 5 inches or one loaf 5¾ x 3¼ inches and one loaf 8 x 4½ inches. I prefer to do the last two since it is always nice to have a loaf of the small size in the freezer for the dainty size slices. Bake according to your size in choosing the time. When a straw inserted in the middle of bread comes clean and dry the bread is done.

Note: You may like to add one-half cup toasted sesame seeds to the above. You may use instant mashed potatoes. Use two tablespoons dry and increase milk to one and one-fourth cups.

Plain Brown Rice Bread

This bread is good as it is written, or as a good base for experimentation. How about a little cinnamon and brown sugar over the top and cooked as a coffee cake? Perhaps a few raisins added to the batter at the last might improve its appeal. Try sprinkling well-drained blueberries through-out the batter by pouring the batter in layers; top with brown sugar and cinnamon if desired.

2 cups brown rice flour	4 eggs
½ cup rice polish	1½ cups milk
1 tablespoon potato flour	1 packet gelatin, softened in ½ cup of your milk, heated to dissolve. Do not boil.
1 teaspoon salt	
2 tablespoons baking powder	
½ cup sugar or less, if desired	½ cup salad oil

Sift flour with other dry ingredients; add eggs, pre-pared milk, and salad oil all at once; stir or beat until blended. Fill greased pans two-thirds full and bake for one hour at 350 degrees. This will make one pan 5¾ x 3¼ inches and one pan 8 x 4½ inches or three of the small-sized pans. The small pan will take forty-five to fifty minutes, the larger size requiring about an hour. Coffee cake will require about forty-five minutes. If you make this into a coffee cake, you may omit the gelatin since it is used as a binder for a better-slicing bread.

Corn Loaf Bread

Use either white or yellow corn meal. The flavor will be slightly different.

¾ cup brown rice flour	2 eggs
¾ cup corn meal	⅔ cup buttermilk
2 tablespoons potato flour	3 tablespoons oil
3 tablespoons sugar	1 teaspoon grated orange peel
3 teaspoons baking powder	
1 teaspoon soda	
½ teaspoon salt	

Sift the dry ingredients together and place them into a mixing bowl. Beat the eggs with the buttermilk in a sepa-rate bowl. Stir in the oil and combine with the dry ingredi-ents. Stir in the grated orange peel. Pour into a loaf pan

4½ x 8½ inches which has been lined with wax paper and
then greased. Bake in a 400 degree oven for fifteen minutes;
reduce heat to 375 degrees and bake twenty to thirty
minutes longer. It should be golden brown and crusty.

Flour Medley Bread

2 cups brown rice flour	½ cup sugar
¼ cup soya flour	3 teaspoons baking powder
¼ cup rice polish	1 teaspoon soda
1 cup rice bran	4 eggs, separated
½ cup corn *flour*	2 cups buttermilk
2 tablespoons potato flour	2 tablespoons cooking oil
1 teaspoon salt	

Sift all the dry ingredients together. Add egg yolks,
buttermilk, and oil. Blend at low speed in your mixer until
well combined. Fold in stiffly-beaten egg whites at the
last. Bake sixty to seventy minutes at 350 degrees.

Crisp Corn Pone

If y'all were raised in the South, you will enjoy this.
If you were not, you will still like it for variety in your
bread stuff diet. The yield is four servings.

1 cup corn meal	1 cup boiling water
½ teaspoon salt	2 teaspoons salad oil

Sift corn meal and salt together into bowl; add boiling
water and stir to form a stiff dough. Dip hands in cold
water, shape dough into flat cakes one-half inch thick.
Place on griddle which has been well greased. Bake in
450 degree oven twenty minutes. Serve hot with butter and
syrup.

Spoon Bread

A little Southern touch!

2 cups milk	4 tablespoons butter
1 cup yellow corn meal	4 eggs, separated
1 teaspoon salt	

Heat milk in double boiler, add corn meal slowly, stirring constantly. Continue cooking and stirring until mixture is thick and smooth. Do not let mixture get too thick. Add the salt and butter and remove from heat to cool slightly. Beat the egg yolks until light and add to the corn meal. Beat the egg whites until stiff but not dry; carefully fold into the corn meal mixture. Pour into a well-buttered casserole and bake in a 375 degree oven thirty-five to forty minutes. It should be puffed and brown on top. Serve with a spoon. Use butter, salt, and pepper. It will serve six.

Spoon Bread

1 cup boiling water	2 teaspoons baking powder
½ cup white corn meal	1 tablespoon soft butter
½ cup milk	3 eggs, well beaten
½ teaspoon salt	

Pour boiling water over corn meal, beating vigorously so that it will be free from lumps. Beat in milk, salt, baking powder, butter, and eggs. Pour into one quart casserole or loaf Pyrex dish. Bake at 400 degrees for thirty-five to forty minutes or until just set. Serve piping hot with butter.

Either one of the above spoon breads makes a delicious casserole when poured over oysters which have been partially drained, dotted generously with butter, salted, and peppered.

Hila's Garlic Grits

Unusual and so good for a buffet dinner.

2 cups hominy grits	4 well-beaten eggs
6 cups water	½ cup margarine or butter
½ cup milk	1 teaspoon salt
2 rolls garlic cheese *or* one 8-ounce package cream cheese and 2 drops oil of garlic	¼ teaspoon pepper
	Parmesan cheese
	Paprika

Cook grits in water as directed on grit package. Add

milk and cheese, mix well; add eggs, margarine, and salt and pepper. Pour into a buttered casserole and sprinkle with Parmesan cheese and paprika (use paprika as you would pepper). Cover casserole and bake at 300 degrees for thirty minutes or until set when tested with knife into the center. It serves eight to ten people.

Boston Brown Bread

We were brought up eating brown bread and baked beans every Saturday night. Even though we have not continued the practice—putting it on the forbidden list when made with wheat—rye and corn flours make it most desirable! It was a happy day when I had an inspiration for making this substitute. The bread is light, moist, and delicious.

1 cup brown rice flour	1 teaspoon baking powder
1 cup corn meal	¼ cup sugar
1 cup rice bran	⅔ cup dark molasses
1 teaspoon salt	1½ cups buttermilk
1 teaspoon potato flour	2 whole eggs
2 teaspoons soda	⅔ cup raisins

If you have saved them, use large size baking powder cans. If not, why not save them in the future? Otherwise, use the slimmest cans you can find. Line the bottoms of the cans with foil or wax paper. Butter the molds thoroughly. Mix and sift dry ingredients, add molasses, buttermilk, and eggs. Fold in raisins. Fill molds two-thirds full; cover tightly. Place on a rack, not directly onto the bottom of your kettle. Keep water half-way up the cans at all times. Boil gently for one and one-half hours.

Prune Bread

A different flavor and texture, delicious for little sandwiches with cream cheese.

1½ cups brown rice flour	1 tablespoon soya flour
½ cup rice polish	3 teaspoons baking powder
1 tablespoon potato flour	

Continued on overleaf

1 cup finely cut cooked prunes	¼ cup salad oil
4 eggs, separated	1 cup milk
¾ cup sugar	2 teaspoons lemon rind
1 teaspoon salt	

Sift the flours three times after measuring to insure even blending. Of the flours, the potato flour especially will give you trouble if it is not blended correctly.

Beat prunes, egg whites, and one-half cup sugar until stiff to form a prune whip. In a second bowl, sift in dry ingredients, including remaining one-fourth cup sugar, add oil, two-thirds cup milk, and lemon rind. Beat one minute at medium speed. Add remaining milk and egg yolks. Beat one more minute. Fold in prune whip. Pour into loaf pans which have been lined with wax paper and greased. This will make one small loaf and one medium-sized loaf. I like to make it this way to have one small loaf for dainty slices and sandwiches. Bake at 350 degrees about fifty minutes for the small loaf and seventy minutes for the medium-sized loaf.

Apricot Bread

1 cup slivered apricots	3 teaspoons baking powder
1 cup brown rice flour	5 tablespoons sugar
¼ cup rice polish	2 eggs
1 teaspoon potato flour	¾ cup sweet milk
½ teaspoon salt	2 tablespoons salad oil

If apricots are quite soft, cut them into fine slivers without cooking; if not, cook very lightly and then cut. Avoid cooking to soft or mushy stage. Sift flour with other dry ingredients, reserving one-fourth cup flour to dredge the fruit; add milk and eggs all at once; add shortening and stir or beat until ingredients are blended; add apricots and stir to blend only. Pour into loaf pan 8 x 4½ inches and bake for sixty minutes at 350 degrees.

Note: Double all ingredients to make two loaves, freeze one. Try not to cut this bread until it has set all day or overnight—it will cut much better.

You will soon find out that there are no wheat-free crackers at the market. There are corn chips and potato chips, but you must watch them for seasoning. The recipes given below are gourmet fare. Yield: four to five dozen, depending upon size.

Sesame Seed Crackers I

1 tablespoon potato flour	½ cup grated Monterrey Jack cheese
1 cup brown rice flour	
½ teaspoon baking powder	or Mozarella
½ cup browned sesame seed	½ cup butter or margarine
4 tablespoons cold water	1 egg

Combine flour, baking powder, seed, and cheese; stir with a fork; add butter, cutting it into the flour mixture as you would for pastry; add egg and water and knead into a ball with your hands. Roll out the dough and cut into squares or circles as you desire. (You may roll out on foil and leave it on the foil for baking.) Brush the tops with melted butter, sprinkle lightly with salt if you wish, and bake at 425 degrees for fifteen minutes or until lightly browned.

Sesame Seed Crackers II

A harder and drier cracker.

1 tablespoon potato flour	⅓ cup sesame seed (browned)
1 cup brown rice flour	
½ teaspoon baking powder	⅓ cup grated Mozarella or Monterrey Jack cheese
½ teaspoon salt	
⅓ cup sesame seed meal	1 egg
	4 tablespoons cold water

Follow directions for Sesame Seed Crackers I, but brush tops with a slightly beaten egg white. Bake at 425 degrees for fifteen minutes or until lightly browned.

Cheese Corn Meal Biscuits

Light and tasty, good with stew.

¾ cup milk
½ cup yellow corn meal
1 cup rice flour
1 tablespoon baking powder
¾ teaspoon salt

1 teaspoon potato flour
3 tablespoons butter
¾ cup grated cheddar cheese
2 eggs

Scald milk and add corn meal. Mix well and cool. Sift together twice the flour, baking powder, salt, and potato flour. Cut the butter into the flour mixture until it resembles fine bread crumbs. Add cheese and eggs to milk-corn meal mixture. Mix thoroughly. Turn out onto a lightly-floured board. Knead two to three minutes. Roll out one-half inch thick. Cut into biscuits; place on greased baking sheet. Bake in a very hot oven at 425 degrees for about fifteen minutes, or until golden brown. Serve warm, split, and buttered.

Corn Sticks

1 cup yellow corn meal
¾ cup boiling water
4 egg yolks

1 tablespoon rice polish
1 teaspoon salt
4 egg whites

Blend corn meal with boiling water and cool. Beat the egg yolks, rice polish, and salt into this mixture. Fold in the beaten egg whites. Dip mixture onto a well-greased cookie sheet and form into sticks. Bake thirty minutes at 350 degrees.

Basic Waffle Recipe

2 cups brown rice
  flour
1 teaspoon salt
1 tablespoon sugar

1 tablespoon baking powder
3 eggs
½ cup cooking oil
1½ cups milk

Sift the dry ingredients together into your mixing bowl. Add the eggs, oil, and milk. Mix at low speed until the batter is free of lumps and smooth, and the egg is completely blended. Rice flour does not toughen with beating as wheat flour does. If you wish, the egg whites may be beaten separately and folded into the batter. Bake at medium heat in your waffle iron. Yield: eight to ten waffles.

Variations of the basic recipe:

Rice Polish Waffles

These are delicate, crispy, and our favorite for strawberry shortcake.

1 cup rice polish	1 tablespoon sugar
1 cup brown rice flour	3 eggs
1 tablespoon baking powder	½ cup oil
1 teaspoon salt	1½ cups milk

This is a crisper waffle than the basic recipe. If you desire a very light and very special waffle, try using four eggs. Mix as with the basic recipe.

Combination Waffles I

1 cup brown rice flour	1 teaspoon salt
½ cup soya flour	3 eggs
½ cup rice polish	½ cup cooking oil
1 tablespoon baking powder	1½ cups milk
1 tablespoon sugar	

Combination Waffles II

1 cup brown rice flour	1 teaspoon salt
½ cup rice bran	3 eggs
½ cup soya flour	½ cup cooking oil
1 tablespoon baking powder	1½ cups milk
1 tablespoon sugar	

Corn Meal Waffles

¾ cup brown rice flour	2 tablespoons sugar
¾ cup corn meal	3 eggs
¾ teaspoon salt	5 tablespoons oil
1 teaspoon soda	1¼ cup yogurt *or* buttermilk
3 teaspoons baking powder	

Sift dry ingredients together. Separate eggs; then add egg yolks, oil, and milk to dry ingredients. Beat the whites until stiff enough to hold soft peaks. Fold into batter. You may use sweet milk and omit soda, but if so, increase baking powder to three and one-half teaspoons. Yield: six to eight waffles.

Gingerbread Waffles

This is actually fine for dessert; variations depend upon your topping.

¼ cup butter or margarine	2 teaspoons baking powder
¼ cup sugar	
2 eggs	1 teaspoon ginger
½ cup molasses	½ teaspoon cinnamon
1 cup natural brown rice flour	¼ teaspoon cloves
¼ cup rice polish or rice bran	½ cup hot water
¼ teaspoon salt	

Cream shortening and sugar until smooth; add eggs and molasses and beat thoroughly; add the sifted dry ingredients and mix smooth. Stir in hot water. Bake on ungreased waffle iron. Makes three to four waffles. They are good topped with orange marmalade, apple sauce, or whipped cream.

Corn Flour Waffles

Very delicate and good.

1 cup corn flour	1 teaspoon salt
1 cup corn meal (yellow)	3 eggs
3 teaspoons baking powder	5 tablespoons oil
2 tablespoons sugar	1½ cups milk

Sift dry ingredients together, add eggs, oil, and milk and beat until well blended. Yield: eight waffles.

Corn—Potato Muffins

1 cup mashed potatoes	2 eggs	1 teaspoon salt
2 tablespoons melted butter	1 cup milk	3 teaspoons baking powder
1 tablespoon sugar	1 cup corn meal	

Have potatoes lump free, then whip; add melted butter, sugar, eggs, and milk. Beat until smooth and completely blended; add corn meal, baking powder, and salt which have been sifted together. Pour into greased muffin tins, filling them about two-thirds full. Bake about forty minutes at 350 degrees. Yield: one dozen muffins.

You can have lots of fun with muffins, so let yourself go! All products made with our flours and baked in small containers improve in texture. I indulge myself and use cupcake liners.

Tea Muffins

1 cup brown rice flour	3 tablespoons sugar
¼ cup rice polish	2 eggs
1 teaspoon potato flour	¾ cup sweet milk
½ teaspoon salt	4 tablespoons safflower oil
3 teaspoons baking powder	*or* other salad oil

Sift flour with other dry ingredients; add milk and eggs all at once; add shortening and stir or beat until ingredients are blended. Fill greased muffin pans two-thirds full and bake at 400 degrees for twenty minutes. Yield: one dozen.

Variations:

(1) Add one-half cup of any of the following: raisins, chopped dates, slivered dried apricots, finely-diced raw apple, chopped and drained cooked prunes, well-drained finely-sliced pineapple. (2) Add one teaspoon grated orange or lemon peel.

Blueberry Muffins

1 cup brown rice flour	4 tablespoons sugar
¼ cup rice polish	2 eggs
1 teaspoon potato flour	¾ cup sweet milk
½ teaspoon salt	4 tablespoons melted butter
3 teaspoons baking powder	Blueberries (about 1 cup)

Sift flour with other dry ingredients; add milk and eggs all at once; add melted butter and stir until the ingredients are blended. Drop one scant tablespoon batter into muffin cup, then drop in some blueberries. Repeat until pan is two-thirds full. If you use canned blueberries, be sure they are well drained. Bake at 400 degrees for twenty minutes. This batter makes one dozen delicious muffins which bake without bleeding blueberries into the batter.

Bran Muffins

¾ cup brown rice flour	1 cup milk
½ teaspoon salt	2 eggs
3 teaspoons baking powder	⅓ cup melted shortening
½ cup brown sugar	(butter or margarine)
1 cup rice bran	

Sift dry ingredients; add milk, eggs, and shortening. Mix until smooth. Bake in greased muffin pans or muffin pan liners until brown or for about fifteen minutes at 425 degrees. Yield: One and one-half dozen muffins.

Corn Muffins

Or make these into corn sticks if you are lucky enough to have the iron corn stick pans!

2 eggs	1 cup brown rice flour
2 tablespoons sugar	1 cup corn meal
⅔ cup milk	3 teaspoons baking powder
½ cup melted butter	½ teaspoon salt

Beat the eggs until light, mix with sugar, milk, and shortening. Sift the flour, corn meal, baking powder, and salt together. Add liquid mixture to the dry ingredients all at once. Blend. Quickly fill greased muffin tins two-thirds full. Bake at 400 degrees for twenty minutes. Yield: twelve muffins.

Note: Two tablespoons finely chopped onion may be added to the batter for variation—especially good with fish.

Flour Medley Muffins

Delicious and nutritious.

¾ cup brown rice flour

½ cup rice polish

½ cup rice bran

1 tablespoon corn meal

3 teaspoons baking powder

½ cup brown sugar

½ teaspoon salt

1 cup milk

2 eggs

⅓ cup melted butter
  or salad oil

Sift flour, salt, baking powder, and sugar; add milk, eggs, and shortening. Mix until smooth. Bake in greased muffin tins until brown or for about fifteen minutes at 425 degrees. Yield: one and one-half dozen muffins.

Molasses—Bran Muffins

2 eggs

¼ cup brown sugar

¼ cup molasses

¾ cup brown rice flour

¾ cup rice bran

¼ cup rice polish

½ teaspoon salt

3 teaspoons baking powder

1 cup milk

⅓ cup melted butter *or*
  margarine

½ cup raisins

Beat eggs with sugar and molasses until light. Add flour and salt which have been sifted together with baking powder; add milk and shortening. Mix until smooth, fold in raisins. Bake at 400 degrees for fifteen to twenty minutes or until lightly browned. Yield: one and one-half dozen muffins.

Variation:

Substitute one-fourth cup soya flour for the rice polish.

Popovers

I did it! I did it! after many failures. For some reason popovers became very important when I could not make them.

Now I make them better than I ever did with wheat flour, and every time I open the oven door to see their golden beauty, I am thrilled.

4 eggs	½ cup rice polish
½ teaspoon salt	1 cup milk
1 teaspoon sugar	2 teaspoons oil (I use saf-
½ cup brown rice flour	flower)

Beat eggs at medium speed a few minutes until frothy. Now add salt, sugar, flour, and half of the milk and mix again at medium speed until smooth. Then add remaining milk and salad oil and beat at low speed just until blended. Pour batter into buttered* Pyrex cups which have been placed on a cookie sheet, filling cups about one-half full. Bake at 475 degrees for fifteen minutes, lower heat to 350 degrees and cook thirty minutes longer. Do not peek while they are cooking. At the very end you may wish to slit the tops with a sharp knife and leave three to four minutes longer to dry out steam. If they are not top hat, you have not followed the directions. Makes eight to twelve popovers, depending upon size of the cups used.

Cheese Torte

This is very delicious, flaky, and flavorous.

1 cup rice flour	2 cups finely grated Cheddar cheese
¼ teaspoon salt	
¼ cup butter or margarine	2 egg yolks, unbeaten

Heat oven to 425 degrees. Sift flour and salt together. Cut butter into flour until it is like coarse meal. In the same way, work in cheese and egg yolks until a firm dough. Refrigerate ten minutes. Roll on lightly floured aluminum

---

*When I say buttered, I use it in a general way. The dictionary states, "any of certain other spreads having a solid consistency like butter." I mean specifically grease with a solid fat. Oil is immediately absorbed into the batter which then allows the batter to stick to the Pyrex cup. By greasing with a solid fat the popover does not stick—if the cup is well greased.

foil as thin as possible. Shape into a ten-inch round. Bake eight to ten minutes.

Cheese Daisies

¾ cup butter	1½ cups brown rice flour
1½ cups grated Cheddar cheese	*or* 1 cup brown rice flour and ½ cup rice polish
¼ cup grated Parmesan cheese	
¾ teaspoon paprika	1 teaspoon salt

Combine the butter, Cheddar, and Parmesan cheese. Sift the flour, paprika, and salt together. Add to the cheese mixture and stir into a well-mixed dough. Put dough in a cookie press, using shapes of your choice, but keep them small. Bake in 350-degree oven for about twelve minutes, or until lightly browned. Yield: approximately three dozen.

Cheese Surprise

1 cup grated Cheddar cheese	Dash cayenne
2 tablespoons melted butter	3 tablespoons milk
½ cup brown rice flour	1 (3 oz.) jar stuffed green olives

Combine all ingredients with the exception of the olives. Pat mixture around each drained olive to cover completely. Bake on a greased cookie sheet at 400 degrees for ten minutes, or until lightly browned. Serve at once. Makes sixteen to eighteen puffs.

Pancakes

When making pancakes don't be afraid to experiment a little. Live dangerously and make mix with buttermilk and soda instead of sweet milk and all baking powder! Make them thin or make them fat. We who live on this diet can not drop in at a supermarket and pick up prepared foods, we must start from the very beginning on every recipe—but we don't have to get into a rut or play just one note.

You will notice that the leavening remains fairly constant in proportion to the flour used. I have found three teaspoons of baking powder or two teaspoons of baking powder and one teaspoon soda to two cups of flour and three eggs the best combination. That seems like a lot of leavening, but that is the need of our flour.

The recipes in several instances are the same as for waffle batter. I often make up batter and alternate between making waffles or pancakes for breakfast.

I always use no less than one cup of brown rice flour to the two cups of flour in the recipe. From there I suit my "fancy" of the moment. Why don't you? Try these flour combinations:

1. One cup brown rice flour, one-half cup rice polish, one-half cup soya flour.

2. One cup brown rice flour, one cup rice polish.

3. One cup brown rice flour, one-half cup rice polish, one-fourth cup soya flour, one-fourth cup rice bran.

4. One cup brown rice flour, one-half cup corn meal, one-half cup rice polish.

In any one of the above, it might suit your schedule to make up a dry mix and store it for speedy use.

Pancakes

Basic Recipe:

1½ cups brown rice flour	1 tablespoon baking powder
½ cup rice polish	1 teaspoon potato flour
1 teaspoon salt	3 whole eggs
1 tablespoon sugar	½ cup cooking oil
	1½ cups milk

Sift the dry ingredients together into your mixing bowl. Add the eggs, oil, and milk. Mix at medium speed until the batter is free of lumps and smooth, and the egg completely blended. Bake at medium heat on your pancake griddle.

Blueberry Pancakes

Use the above recipe. Drain blueberries thoroughly. As

you drop batter onto griddle, drop four or five blueberries
onto it. By using this method, you will not have the berries
bleeding into your batter.

Variations:

Fold in any of the following: bits of crisp bacon, diced
leftover ham, thoroughly cooked sausage, well-drained pineapple, well-drained cooked corn.

Rice Bran Pancakes

1 cup brown rice flour	1 teaspoon salt
1 cup rice bran	3 whole eggs
2 teaspoons baking powder	½ cup cooking oil
1 teaspoon soda	1½ cups buttermilk
1 tablespoon sugar	

Sift dry ingredients; make a well in the center, add
eggs, oil, and buttermilk and mix until smooth. Bake at
medium heat on an ungreased griddle.

Corn Meal and Rice Pancakes

1 cup corn meal	1 tablespoon melted butter
¾ teaspoon soda	½ cup cooked rice
1 teaspoon salt	1 cup buttermilk
1 teaspoon sugar	2 egg whites, beaten
2 egg yolks, beaten	

Mix dry ingredients. Combine with egg yolks, butter,
rice, and half of the buttermilk. Blend, then add the rest of
the buttermilk. Fold in beaten whites. Fry on lightly greased
griddle.

Hominy Pancakes

1½ cups cooked hominy	½ cup corn meal
2 tablespoons melted butter	¼ cup milk for thick batter,
2 eggs, separated	*or* ½ cup milk for thinner
½ to ¾ teaspoon salt	cake
3 teaspoons baking powder	

Cook hominy according to cereal instructions. While hot, add butter, then cool to warm; add egg yolks and beat; add salt, baking powder, and corn meal, which have been sifted together; add milk; when desired thickness of batter has been achieved, fold in beaten egg whites. Fry on lightly greased hot griddle and serve with butter and syrup.

French Pancakes or Crepes

3 eggs	1 tablespoon potato flour
Pinch of salt	1 cup sweet milk
½ cup brown rice flour	1 teaspoon baking powder
¼ cup rice polish	

You may wonder at using baking powder with crepes. Remember, our flour does not help in the leavening process. For this reason I like to help the batter a bit. If you like the crepe better nearly unleavened, you are on your own. Separate the eggs, and add the salt to the yolks. Alternately add the flour which has been sifted together twice with the baking powder, then add the milk. Fold in the beaten whites. Drop on a buttered griddle and cook until golden brown.

Crepe Suzette Sauce

6 lumps sugar	¼ cup powdered sugar
1 orange	2 tablespoons brandy flavoring
1 lemon	
¼ cup butter	2 tablespoons cointreau flavoring
¼ teaspoon vanilla	

Rub lumps of sugar on outside of orange and lemon for flavor and color; squeeze juice from orange. Place butter in hot chafing dish, add prepared lump sugar, orange juice, and vanilla. Reduce the heat. Add crepes and cook until sauce is reduced to heavy syrup. Fold crepes in quarters, sprinkle with powdered sugar and pour brandy and cointreau flavoring over them. Ignite and serve. You may use equal parts Curacao and Grand Marnier. When making crepes for this, it is nice to add one teaspoon grated lemon or orange rind to the batter.

Orange Pancakes

Delicious and different!

3 eggs, separated	Dash pepper
1 teaspoon grated orange peel	3 tablespoons milk
	⅓ cup brown rice polish
½ teaspoon salt	½ teaspoon potato flour

Beat the egg yolks until thick. Add orange peel, salt, pepper, and milk. Beat the egg whites until they hold peaks, but not until they are stiff. Fold egg yolks into the whites; fold rice polish and potato flour, which have been sifted together, into egg mixture. Bake on medium griddle about four minutes for each side or until golden brown. Do not have griddle too hot as this is *egg*. Makes about twelve fluffy little cakes which can be served with the topping of your choice—try orange marmalade.

Cheese Blintzes

These are wonderful for breakfast or for dessert, especially when topped with fresh or frozen berries and sour cream.

4 eggs	1 teaspoon potato flour
1 cup cottage cheese	1 tablespoon sugar
1 cup sour cream	½ teaspoon salt
1 cup brown rice flour	1 teaspoon baking powder

Beat eggs. Add cottage cheese and sour cream and beat well. Sift dry ingredients together and add; beat until thick. Bake on buttered griddle.

For dessert: While hot, place a heaping teaspoon of cottage cheese in center of each pancake. Roll up and top with sour cream and fruit of your choice. Or spread with jam, top with cottage cheese, and roll. Yield: approximately eight to ten.

Sara's Noodles

Sara has been on a wheat-free diet for eight years. She developed this delicious recipe to fill the void left when wheat flour noodles were denied to her. It is a great help for soups and casseroles.

2 eggs	2 packed tablespoons corn-
1 large tablespoon condensed	starch
milk	All the rice flour the mixture
1 teaspoon salt	will take

Beat the eggs well; add the condensed milk and salt; sift the flour and cornstarch together and add to the egg-milk mixture; knead this thoroughly; roll out in a thin sheet; then cut into strips about one-quarter-inch wide (it may be necessary to cut them just a bit wider if they give you trouble in handling). *Let dry,* put into a plastic bag and freeze. Use as you wish. Yield: four to six servings.

Note: This is another example of a product with no-stretch strength because of the lack of gluten. If you cut the noodles on your board and then leave them undisturbed for four or five hours or even overnight and then gently lift them into the container of your choice they can be handled quite successfully. If you freeze them before using this step, it increases the ease of handling.

Section 4

CAKES, FILLINGS, AND FROSTINGS

One of my cookbooks states very positively, "When it comes to cakes, even the experienced cook cannot improvise successfully." I did not read that until long after I had improvised with gusto and cooked strictly in the empirical manner. In fact, some of my trial-and-error cooking encompassed a few "hunches." Of course, I had a launching point from a favorite recipe which used wheat flour. I knew what I wanted in the way of texture, lightness, flavor, and togetherness.

I also kept these facts in mind: when using wheat flour or flour with gluten, approximately one and one-half teaspoons of baking powder per cup of sifted flour are used.

If baking soda is used, one-half teaspoon to one cup sour milk or buttermilk, or one-half cup molasses, gives as much leavening power as two teaspoons baking powder. Baking soda should be mixed and sifted with the flour and supplemented with the additional baking powder needed to leaven the amount of flour called for in the recipe. If added to the liquid, much of the gas escapes as soon as the two are combined.

I use a flour with no gluten to stretch and hold the air as it is beaten in, or as it is released by leavening. My flour needs increased leavening as it does not help itself.

I learned that eggs hold air as the protein in the egg stretches and coagulates on heating; that eggs beaten separately increase volume when folded into the batter. Even if the beaten egg whites cannot be folded in because of the stiffness of the batter, but must be beaten in, the texture is improved somewhat.

Eggs act as a binder. They provide togetherness. Did

37

you ever use egg white for glue when you were caught without glue and needed some at once?

I found that potato flour in very small quantities is a
great help. It provides togetherness and refines texture. It
is a starch and must be thoroughly blended with the other
flours used to prevent lumping or balling in spots. For cakes
I always sift the potato flour three times with the dry ingredients to insure an even distribution of the potato flour.
Although a little improves texture, too much gives heaviness.

You will note that chocolate is used frequently. If
your dieter also has a sensitivity to chocolate, health food
stores or the El Molino Mills of Alhambra, California, sell
carob. This is a very good tasting, very chocolate-tasting
substitute for the actual chocolate.

Zabaglione Cake

Luscious, with a mingling of flavors to tickle the
taste buds.

6 eggs, separated	1 teaspoon baking powder
1 cup sugar	1 tablespoon potato flour,
2 tablespoons water	plus brown rice flour to
Grated rind of 1 lemon	fill 1 cup——Sift three
¼ teaspoon salt	times

Beat yolks, sugar, water, lemon rind, and salt until light
and fluffy—fifteen to twenty minutes—at high speed. Now
carefully fold in flour a little at a time. Beat whites until
soft peaks form. Gently, but thoroughly, fold the whites
into the yolk mixture. Pour into three 8-inch cake pans
lined with wax paper which have been greased and lightly
dusted with flour. Bake at 325 degrees for forty-five minutes
or until done. Remove from oven and invert. When just
warm, loosen edges and remove from pan. Peel off the paper
and cool. Put layers together with the following filling.

Sauce	Filling
1 cup sugar	1 egg
¾ cup water	¾ cup sugar
Peel from 1 lemon and 1	¼ cup flour
orange	Grated rind and juice of 1
3 cloves	orange
2 teaspoons rum extract	1 cup heavy cream, whipped

Sauce: Place all ingredients except rum extract in a sauce pan and simmer gently for twenty minutes or until the consistency of a thin syrup. Remove from heat and add rum flavoring. Remove cloves, orange, and lemon peel.

Filling: Place all filling ingredients except cream in the top of a double boiler and heat, stirring until thickened and smooth. Cool, then fold in whipped cream. Brush two cake layers liberally with sauce, then spread with filling and put all layers together. Now brush sides of cake with one cup of confectioner's sugar, which has been beaten smooth with one egg white and one-half teaspoon lemon juice. You may decorate the cake top with fruit or clusters of fresh berries.

Orange Spongecake

8 eggs, separated	1 tablespoon grated orange
¼ teaspoon salt	rind
1 teaspoon Cream of Tartar	1 cup brown rice flour
1⅓ cups sugar	1 tablespoon potato flour
¼ cup orange juice	1 teaspoon baking powder

Whip the egg whites with salt until foamy. Add Cream of Tartar and beat until stiff. Gradually add two-thirds cup sugar, beating well after each addition. Beat egg yolks with remaining two-thirds cup sugar until very thick and yellow. Beat in orange juice and rind. Fold yolk mixture into whites; sift flour and baking powder three times and fold into egg mixture very carefully. Pour into ungreased 10-inch tube pan and bake sixty to seventy minutes at 325 degrees. Invert pan on rack to cool. Do not remove from pan until cool. Frost or cover with whipped cream.

Chocolate or Cocoa Roll

5 eggs, separated	1 teaspoon vanilla
½ cup sugar	½ pint whipping cream
3 tablespoons cocoa	or filling of your
1 teaspoon baking powder	choice

Beat egg yolks and sugar, add cocoa and vanilla, fold in stiffly beaten egg whites and bake in 350-degree oven for fifteen minutes in a jelly roll pan approximately 9 x 13 inches. Be sure to beat the yolks and sugar until very light. Be sure to line the pan with a well-greased wax paper. When baked, remove from oven and immediately cover the top with a faintly damp cloth. Cool three to five minutes, then loosen from tin and invert over a clean dry towel which has been sprinkled with powdered sugar. Gently remove wax paper from bottom of cake, cut away any crusty parts, and gently roll, using towel to support cake as you go. Roll several inches of your towel into the first turn. When cool, unroll, spread with filling, reroll and serve.

Note: No, this is not an error, there is no flour in this roll!

Variation:

If you wish, you may use three tablespoons Carob powder as a substitute for the cocoa. All else is the same. This is delicious.

Sponge Jelly Roll

This is a quickie. It is delicious with whipped cream, jam, or one of the "specials" for a filling.

5 eggs	½ cup brown rice flour
¼ teaspoon salt (scant)	plus
⅓ cup sugar	1 teaspoon potato flour
1 teaspoon vanilla	1 teaspoon Cream of Tartar

Beat the eggs, salt, and sugar together until very light and thickened. Do not stint on this, but rather beat until the mixture comes to the top of your small (one and one-half quart) mixer bowl. Sift the dry ingredients three times, and very gently fold into the egg mixture. Have ready a jelly roll pan approximately 9 x 13 inches, which has been lined with wax paper, greased and floured. Spread the mixture evenly on top of the greased paper and bake for twelve to fifteen minutes in a 375 degree oven or until just firm. Remove from oven, cover with a faintly damp cloth for five minutes; invert on a dry cloth which has been liberally sprinkled with powdered sugar. Carefully cut away any crisp edges, gently remove wax paper and roll using the towel to support the cake. (I roll several inches of the towel into the roll to help round out the first turn). When the cake is cool and you are ready, unroll carefully and fill with your choice. Reroll and dust with powdered sugar, or you may frost if you wish.

Lemon Filling

This is a base filling, although it may be used alone sparingly. It makes a very delicious filling for sponge jelly roll or a sponge cake when used half and half with whipped cream.

4 lemons, juice and rind	6 egg yolks
1 cup sugar	2 whole eggs
½ cup butter	

Combine lemon juice and rind, sugar, and butter in heavy saucepan. Place over low heat until mixture is boiling and sugar is dissolved. Beat yolks and whole eggs in a bowl until they are combined. Now, continue to beat with a whisk and pour some of the boiling liquid into the eggs, pouring in very slowly. When lemon mixture, without the rind, is completely blended, put back over low heat and stir briskly until mixture becomes thick, or for about five minutes. Remove from the heat, but continue to stir for about five more minutes. This makes about one quart. It will keep for a very long time in your refrigerator.

Spongecake

Makes a good launching pad for many desserts. It is nice to keep in the freezer for sudden needs. It's as good as the corner grocery is for non-dieters.

½ cup brown rice flour	1¼ cups sugar
1 tablespoon potato flour plus enough rice polish to fill ½ cup	½ cup water
	6 eggs, separated
	¼ teaspoon salt
1 teaspoon Cream of Tartar	1 teaspoon vanilla
1½ teaspoon baking powder	

Sift the flour three times with the Cream of Tartar and baking powder. Mix sugar and water and bring to a boil; boil until the syrup just spins a thread. *Don't* work for a spinning wheel thread! Beat the egg whites and salt until stiff, but not dry. Pour hot syrup over the egg whites slowly, beating as you pour. Beat until cool, then add vanilla. Fold in the egg yolks which have been beaten until thick and lemon-colored. Fold in the dry ingredients very gently. Pour into layer cake tins which have been lined with wax paper. Bake thirty-five to forty minutes in a 325-degree oven.

Marian's Whipped Cream Frosting

Delicious Topping.

1 pint whipping cream	1 teaspoon vanilla
8 tablespoons Droste Cocoa	¼ cup sugar

Mix ingredients; refrigerate overnight, and whip.

Dutch Cream

Although not as good as Marian's, this makes a fast substitute when pressed for time.

½ pint cream, whipped	3 tablespoons confectioner's sugar
3 heaping tablespoons Baker's Instant Dutch chocolate Flavored Mix	1 teaspoon vanilla

Whip the cream until it holds its shape, add Mix and sugar, whip and add vanilla. Spread over two layers of sponge cake.

Fudge Cake

A real fudge cake, moist, and rich.

½ cup beaten mashed potatoes*	½ cup rice polish
½ cup butter	2 teaspoons baking powder
1 cup sugar	1 teaspoon soda
4 eggs, separated	¼ teaspoon salt
3 ounces bitter chocolate	¾ cup buttermilk
1½ cups brown rice flour	1 teaspoon vanilla

Cook potatoes and beat until absolutely smooth and fluffy. Cream butter, add sugar and egg yolks; beat until light and fluffy. Add potatoes and melted chocolate. Mix and sift dry ingredients and add alternately with milk to the creamed mixture. Add vanilla and fold in egg whites which have been beaten to hold peaks, but are not dry. Bake in layer pans at 350 degrees for about twenty-five minutes.

Frosting

This is a wonderful frosting and easy to make! Put the following ingredients into a saucepan of medium size.

2 ounces bitter chocolate	4 tablespoons butter
1½ cups sugar	1 tablespoon corn syrup
7 tablespoons milk	¼ teaspoon salt

Bring slowly to a full rolling boil, stirring constantly. Boil very rapidly for one minute. Be sure that it is a full rolling boil. If the weather is humid, increase the time one-half minute. Cool to lukewarm, add one teaspoon vanilla and beat until thick enough to spread.

*You may use Instant Mashed Potatoes—just follow the directions on the box, or use dry and increase the buttermilk to one and one-fourth cups.

Chocolate Log

This is very rich, a truly melt-in-your mouth morsel!

5 eggs	1 teaspoon baking powder
½ cup sugar	2 tablespoons cocoa
1 tablespoon potato flour plus enough brown rice flour to make ⅓ cup	¼ teaspoon salt

Beat the eggs and sugar until thick and foamy. Sift together the dry ingredients and very carefully fold into the egg mixture. Have ready a jelly roll pan which has been greased, lined with paper, and greased heavily again. Spread the batter gently into the 9 x 14 inch pan, making it even, and bake at 375 degrees for ten minutes, or until firm. Turn cake out onto a clean towel sprinkled with sugar, after carefully loosening from tin, and gently peel off the paper from the bottom. Cut off any crisp edges. Roll up the cake, using the towel to help hold it as you roll. Wrap in the towel and cool completely. Carefully unroll and spread evenly, but not too heavily, with apricot jam. Reroll.

Frosting

3 egg yolks	2 tablespoons rum or 1 teaspoon rum flavoring
1 cup sugar	1 ounce bitter chocolate (grated)
½ cup water	
½ cup butter	1 teaspoon instant coffee

Beat egg yolks until light and fluffy. Cook sugar and water until it forms a light thread. Add butter, instant coffee, and grated chocolate, and let the mixture boil up once more. Just that and no more, with butter cut into thin slices so that it will melt quickly. Pour onto egg yolks, beating constantly. Continue beating until thick and cold, then spread over the log. It is nice to score frosting to simulate a log.

Peppermint-Rum Fluff

I needed a "special" dessert quickly one day and had

to use the materials on hand. This recipe is a simple modification of "Grasshopper," and is very delicious. I used it to fill the chocolate roll which also can be made quickly and easily.

1 envelope gelatin
½ cup water
½ cup sugar
Pinch of salt
3 eggs, separated

½ cup milk
1 teaspoon peppermint extract
1 teaspoon rum flavoring
½ pint cream

Sprinkle gelatin over water in a medium saucepan. Add one-fourth cup sugar, salt, egg yolks, and milk and stir until thoroughly blended. Place over low heat and continue stirring until gelatin dissolves and mixture thickens slightly. Remove from heat and cool, add flavoring, and chill, stirring frequently. Beat with beater until light and fluffy. Meanwhile, beat whites until stiff but not dry. Gradually add remaining one-fourth cup sugar and beat until very stiff. Fold in gelatin mixture and fold in whipped cream. Chill until firm.

Prune Cake

A different approach and so good!

1 cup finely cut cooked prunes
4 eggs, separated
1½ cups sugar
2¼ cups sifted brown rice flour

1 tablespoon potato flour
3 teaspoons baking powder
1 teaspoon salt
¼ cup vegetable oil
1 cup milk
2 teaspoons lemon rind

Beat prunes, egg whites, and one-half cup sugar until stiff. In second bowl sift in remaining sugar and other dry ingredients, add oil, two-thirds cup milk, and lemon rind. Beat one minute at medium speed of mixer. Add remaining milk and egg yolks. Beat one more minute, then fold in prune whip. Pour into layer cake pans which have been lined with wax paper. Bake thirty-five minutes at 350 degrees, until toothpick comes out clean. Fill and frost with whipped cream or seven-minute frosting—either frosting is excellent with this cake.

Dorothy's Applesauce Cake

My sister is a wonderful cook, so naturally I had to adapt some of her recipes for our use.

1 cup sugar	1 teaspoon cinnamon
½ cup butter	½ teaspoon cloves
3 eggs, beaten	1 teaspoon soda
1 cup apple sauce	½ teaspoon salt
1 cup brown rice flour	1 square chocolate (optional)
2 tablespoons potato flour with enough rice polish to fill one-half cup	1 cup seedless raisins

If you use chocolate, you may omit cloves, cinnamon, and raisins for a different flavor.

Cream sugar and shortening, add eggs, and beat until light and fluffy. Add applesauce, and gradually beat in flour and other dry ingredients which have been sifted together three times. Fold in raisins. Bake at 325 degrees for fifty minutes in an 8 x 8 x 2 inch pan. Frost with brown sugar frosting.

Brown Sugar Frosting

1 cup brown sugar   ½ cup butter·

Place in saucepan over direct heat and stir, cooking about ten minutes until it melts and browns just a little. Remove from fire and add the following: one cup white sugar and one-half cup milk. Cook to soft ball stage, cool, add one teaspoon vanilla, and beat until spreading consistency.

German Chocolate Cake

How does the slogan go, "Six out of seven . . . ." I tried this cake on seven people for fun; one noticed a difference from the regular wheat flour cake.

1 package German chocolate   1 teaspoon Cream of Tartar
½ cup boiling water   ½ teaspoon salt
1 cup butter   2⅓ cups flour before sifting
1¾ cups sugar   (brown rice flour)
6 eggs   3 teaspoons baking powder
1 cup buttermilk   1 teaspoon soda
1 teaspoon vanilla   2 tablespoons potato flour

Melt German chocolate in boiling water; cool. Cream butter with sugar, add egg yolks, one at a time, beating thoroughly after each addition. Add the chocolate mixture, vanilla, and salt. Sift together three times the measured flour, baking powder, soda, and potato flour; add this alternately, beating well after each addition, with one cup buttermilk, to the chocolate mixture; beat until smooth and fluffy. Fold in beaten whites. Pour into three layer cake pans which have been lined with wax paper and greased. Bake at 350 degrees for thirty to forty minutes. You may like to use one-half package German chocolate and one square bitter chocolate. If you like a reddish color to your chocolate cakes, add a few drops of red vegetable coloring. Also makes wonderful cupcakes.

Frost with this recipe from the Baker's German Chocolate Wrapper, omitting nuts.

Combine one cup evaporated milk, one cup sugar, three egg yolks, one-half cup butter, one teaspoon vanilla. Cook and stir over medium heat until thickened, about twelve minutes. Add one and one-third cups Angel Flake coconut. Beat until thick enough to spread. Or:

Mocha Fudge Frosting

My favorite, which gives a delectable flavor to the cake.

Melt one-half bar German chocolate with one and one-half cups sugar, seven tablespoons milk, four tablespoons butter, one tablespoon corn syrup (Karo), a pinch of salt, and one teaspoon instant coffee. Bring slowly to a full rolling boil, stirring constantly, and boil briskly one minute, or until it makes a soft ball when dropped in cold water. Cook to lukewarm, add one teaspoon vanilla, and beat until ready to spread. It is especially elegant to top the cake with quartered marshmallows as soon as it comes from the oven, and can be removed from the pans. The marshmallows melt slightly. Then frost the cake.

Cheese Cake

Whip cheese most thoroughly for smoothness.

4 eggs	½ pint whipping cream
1 cup sugar	1½ pounds cottage cheese
¼ teaspoon salt	3 tablespoons brown rice
½ lemon, juice and grated rind	flour
	1 teaspoon vanilla (optional)

Beat whole eggs with sugar until light. Add salt, lemon, and, if desired, vanilla. Stir cream in well, then add cheese and flour whipped together, and put through sieve. Stir until smooth and pour into crumb-lined form. Sprinkle crumbs over the top. Bake at 325 degrees for one hour. Turn off heat and let stand in oven for one hour or until cool.

For Crust:

2 cups crumbs from sesame seed cookies	¼ cup sugar
	½ cup butter

Roll cookie crumbs fine; mix with the other ingredients. Set aside three-fourths cup of the mixture to sprinkle over the top of the cake. Butter well a 9-inch spring form pan and spread and press crumbs on bottom and sides of the form. Or:

2 cups crumbs from basic waffle	1 cup sugar
¼ cup soft butter	¼ teaspoon cinnamon

Dry waffles in oven until crisp throughout. Roll into fine crumbs. Butter spring form pan generously; spread and press crumbs on bottom and sides. If necessary, use more butter.

Section 5

COOKIES, THE INDISPENSABLE SWEET

I think that cookies are the easiest thing to make with our flours. The cake-type cookie requires the adjustments for togetherness and leavening. The drop cookie needs help for togetherness and to avoid any grittiness. However, because of its very small size, the problems are minimized. The recipes included here were mostly favorites when made with wheat flour and continue to be favorites now made with rice or soya flour. Incidentally, the slightly nutty flavor of soya flour is very pleasing in a cookie.

Rolled and sliced cookies are a problem just as pie crust is, but who has time to make rolled cookies anyway?

Fruit Cookies

A delicious cookie for Christmas or any time. Apricots and chocolate are interesting companions.

$2/3$ cup condensed milk	1 teaspoon baking powder
2 lightly beaten eggs	1 small jar candied orange
$1/2$ cup margarine, melted	$1/2$ cup white raisins
$1/2$ cup sugar	$1/2$ 6-ounce package chocolate
$3/4$ cup brown rice flour	niblets
$3/4$ cup soya flour	8-10 apricots cut fine

Put milk, eggs, margarine, and sugar together in mixing bowl and blend, add flour and baking powder, which have been sifted together, and blend until smooth. Fold in the fruits and chocolate niblets. Bake at 375 degrees ten to twelve minutes or until browned. Yield: approximately five to six dozen.

Fruit Balls

My husband calls these "inviting, fattening, and delicious."

49

½ cup butter	1 tablespoon chopped ginger
½ cup brown sugar	½ cup browned sesame seed
½ cup white sugar	½ cup mixed candied fruit
1 teaspoon rum flavoring	1 cup soya flour
1 egg	1 cup brown rice flour

Cream shortening, add sugar, and continue creaming. Add flavoring, egg, fruit and sesame seed, then add flour. Shape into small balls and bake on lightly greased pan for fifteen minutes at 375 degrees, or until lightly browned. Yield: four dozen.

Ida's Sesame Seed Cookies

These are very much a glamour cookie, with just the right amount of delicacy and crispness for a tea party.

¼ cup butter	½ cup sesame seed, browned lightly in a heavy pan until the desired golden brown, or spread on a cookie sheet and browned in a 350-degree oven for about ten minutes.
1 cup brown sugar	
1 egg	
4 tablespoons soya flour	
¼ teaspoon vanilla	

Cream butter and brown sugar; add egg and beat until light and fluffy; add other ingredients and blend. Grease cookie sheet very lightly with oil. Then sprinkle with rice flour and hit the bottom of the sheet sharply from the under side to distribute the flour evenly. Tip off excess flour. Drop one-fourth to one-half teaspoon batter onto sheets, spacing to allow spread of cookie as it heats. Bake five to eight minutes at 375 degrees or until golden brown. Remove cookies from pan quickly with a clean, sharp spatula. Repeat pan preparation for all baking. Yield: approximately nine dozen two-inch wafers.

German Chocolate Brownies

¼ cup butter, melted with 1 bar of German chocolate	1 tablespoon potato flour	2 tablespoons rice flour to dredge fruit
¾ cup sugar	1 teaspoon baking powder	½ cup diced candied citron *or* raisins *or* candied orange peel
2 eggs	¼ teaspoon salt	
⅔ cup soya flour	1½ teaspoons vanilla	

Combine chocolate and butter mixture with sugar; add eggs and beat until light and fluffy. Sift in dry ingredients, add vanilla, and blend. Lightly fold in flour dredged citron or raisins. Pour into greased 8 x 8 x 2 inch baking pan and bake at 350 degrees for twenty-five minutes, or until brownies are firm and begin to pull away from the sides of the pan. Cut into two-inch squares. Yield: sixteen squares.

Variation:

You may use bitter chocolate—one square plus one-half bar German Chocolate or as your taste dictates. You may also substitute an equal amount of carob if you are allergic to chocolate.

Chocolate Chip Cookies

A universal favorite adjusted to our use!

½ cup butter	½ cup brown rice flour
½ cup brown sugar	1 teaspoon baking powder
½ cup white sugar	¼ teaspoon salt
1 egg	1 teaspoon vanilla
½ cup soya flour plus 1 tablespoon	1 package chocolate chips (6 ounces)
1 tablespoon potato flour	

Blend the butter and sugar until creamy; add the egg and beat until fluffy; sift the dry ingredients and mix until smooth; add vanilla; gently fold in chocolate chips. Drop by teaspoon onto greased cookie sheet. Bake at 375 degrees ten to twelve minutes or until brown. Yield: four dozen.

Variation 1:

If you are allergic to chocolate, but hungry for the taste, chop up an equal amount of carob and fold into your batter.

Variation 2:

Omit chocolate and add raisins and dates; or dates and coconut or candied fruit; about one tablespoon candied ginger is delicious with the candied fruit, or add one-half cup dehydrated mince meat.

Variation 3:

Add one-half cup raisins.

Variation 4:

Use all soya flour or use one-half cup brown rice flour and one-half cup rice polish plus one tablespoon.

Basic Cookie

If you find yourself with three egg whites to use up, try this cookie recipe.

½ cup sugar	1 tablespoon potato flour
½ cup butter	¼ teaspoon salt
3 egg whites	2 teaspoons grated lemon
½ cup soya flour	rind
½ cup brown rice flour	1 teaspoon lemon juice

Cream butter and sugar together until fluffy. Beat in egg whites, one at a time, beating very well after each addition. Sift dry ingredients together and mix in thoroughly, then stir in lemon. Drop cookies from teaspoon onto greased baking sheet. Leave about one inch between them. Bake about seven minutes at 400 degrees. Yield: four dozen.

Variation 1:

Substitute rice polish flour for soya flour.

Variation 2:

Add one cup coconut to basic recipe, using either lemon or vanilla as flavoring.

Variation 3:

Increase flour by adding one-fourth cup brown rice flour, make batter into balls, dip in egg white, and roll in coconut.

Variation 4:

Substitute brown sugar for white and vanilla for lemon. Fold in one cup chocolate niblets and one-half cup chopped or sliced dates.

Cherry Buttons

⅓ cup butter or margarine	1 cup soya flour
½ cup sugar	¼ teaspoon salt
1 teaspoon grated lemon peel	1 teaspoon baking powder
1 teaspoon vanilla	½ cup chopped white raisins
1 well-beaten egg	1½ cup crushed Rice Krinkles
1½ tablespoons milk	Candied cherries

Cream shortening and sugar thoroughly; add lemon peel, vanilla, egg, and milk; beat thoroughly. Add sifted dry ingredients, and stir in the raisins. Drop from teaspoon into crushed Rice Krinkles, and toss lightly to coat. Arrange on greased cookie sheet. Top with candied cherry. Bake at 375 degrees for about twelve minutes. Yield: about two and one-half dozen cookies.

Chocolate Chip and Coconut Cookies

These are fudgy but crisp. A different texture!

½ cup butter	½ cup brown rice flour
½ cup sugar	½ cup soya flour
¼ cup brown sugar	1 teaspoon baking powder
1 egg	½ teaspoon salt
1½ squares unsweetened chocolate	1 package chocolate niblets
1 teaspoon vanilla	1 cup Angel Flake coconut

Cream soft butter, white and brown sugar, egg, melted

chocolate, and vanilla until fluffy. Sift together flour, baking powder, and salt and mix into chocolate mixture. Stir in package of chocolate niblets and coconut. Drop from a teaspoon onto greased cookie sheet, about two inches apart. Bake at 375 degrees, twelve to fourteen minutes. Let cookies cool a minute or so before removing from tin. Yield: about four dozen cookies.

Ginger Date Cookies

The ginger gives an unusual taste with dates and sesame—a little exotic!

½ cup butter or margarine	¾ teaspoon salt
1 cup brown sugar	½ teaspoon baking powder
1 egg	1 teaspoon vanilla
½ cup brown rice flour plus 2 tablespoons	2 tablespoons very finely chopped candied ginger
½ cup rice polish	1 cup dates, sliced small
½ cup soya flour	½ cup sesame seed (lightly browned)

Cream butter and sugar together thoroughly. Add egg and beat until fluffy. Sift flour with salt and baking powder and blend into creamed mixture. Stir in vanilla; fold in fruit. Shape into balls by pushing dough into sesame seed and rolling into ball. The dough will be quite soft and needs to be handled lightly. Place on greased and floured baking sheet. Bake at 375 degrees about ten minutes. Yield: about three dozen cookies.

Date Balls

A cross between a cookie and candy.

2 cups Post's Rice Krinkles	2 tablespoons honey
1 cup sliced dates, quartered	1 tablespoon butter
½ cup sesame seed meal	3 teaspoons lemon juice
	Confectioner's sugar

Put dates and Rice Krinkles through meat grinder. Mix

with other ingredients and knead into balls. Roll in powdered
sugar. Makes about thirty balls.

Layer Date Bars

A favorite originally made with oatmeal and, naturally,
wheat flour. Too good to abandon, here is the substitute.

2 cups ground Puffed Rice	1½ cups brown rice
½ cup butter or margarine	flour
1 cup firmly packed brown	¼ teaspoon salt
sugar	1 teaspoon soda

Using your coarse attachment, grind enough Puffed
Rice to make two generous cups. Cream butter and sugar
thoroughly. Sift flour with salt and soda and add to first
mixture; add Puffed Rice and mix to a crumb-like texture.
Place one-half in a 9 x 13 inch cookie pan which has been
lined with wax or brown paper and greased; pat down firmly.
Spread with date filling given below, top with remaining
crumbs, and pat smooth. Bake in a 350-degree oven for
thirty minutes, or until delicately browned. Cut into bars.
Makes about twenty bars.

Date Filling

1 pound pitted, cut dates	1 cup water
1 cup sugar	

Combine ingredients and cook until consistency of jam.

Fruit Bar Cookies

½ cup butter or margarine	1 teaspoon baking powder
1 cup light brown sugar	½ teaspoon cinnamon
1 egg	2 tablespoons milk
1 teaspoon vanilla	¼ cup chopped candied
¼ teaspoon rum flavoring	orange peel
¾ cup brown rice flour	¼ cup chopped candied
¾ cup soya flour	lemon peel
	½ cup seedless white raisins

Cream butter and sugar, add egg and beat until light

and fluffy. Add flavoring, then add sifted dry ingredients alternately with milk and mix well. Fold in fruit. Pour into greased 9-inch square pan. Bake at 350 degrees for thirty minutes. Cut into bars.

Fig or Date Bars

3 eggs	1 tablespoon potato flour
¾ cup sugar	½ teaspoon salt
1 teaspoon vanilla	2 teaspoons baking powder
½ cup brown rice flour	1½ cups chopped figs or
½ cup rice polish	dates

Beat eggs until light. Add sugar and vanilla and beat until thick. Add sifted dry ingredients and mix well. Stir in fruit. Bake in shallow 9½ x 13½ inch pan which has been lined with wax paper and greased. Bake at 350 degrees for thirty minutes. Yield: four dozen. You may roll in powdered sugar for added glamour.

Coconut Macaroons

Chewy and moist.

¼ cup rice polish	14-ounce package Angel Flake
¼ cup soya flour	coconut
½ teaspoon salt	3 tablespoons dark Karo
⅔ cup milk (1 can)	1½ teaspoons vanilla
	½ teaspoon almond flavoring

Sift the dry ingredients together, mix thoroughly with the remaining ingredients. Drop from a teaspoon onto baking sheet which has been lightly greased and floured. Bake at 325 degrees for twenty minutes or until lightly browned. Yield: four dozen.

Variation 1:

Divide mixture in half before adding almond flavoring. To one-half, add one square melted bitter chocolate, to other half, add one-fourth teaspoon almond flavoring. (Two squares of semi-sweet chocolate may be used in place of the bitter.)

Variation 2:

Use basic recipe; add one-half cup white raisins.

Variation 3:

Use basic recipe and your imagination!

Apricot Cookies

A spritz-type cookie filled with apricot jam.

Step I:

Use apricot jam which has been prepared in this manner:

1 pound dried apricots	1 tablespoon grated orange rind
1½ cups sugar	
6 tablespoon lemon juice	1 tablespoon grated lemon rind

Soak the apricots overnight in cold water barely covering them. The next day, cover and cook until puffy and tender. Mash, and add the remaining ingredients and cook, stirring constantly until thick and waxy. Cool and use any excess amount to serve as a jam.

Step II:

½ cup butter	1 egg
¼ cup brown sugar	1 cup soya flour
⅓ cup white sugar	1 cup brown rice flour
¼ teaspoon salt	½ cup sesame seed (optional)
1 teaspoon vanilla	

Cream shortening, add sugar and continue creaming. Add remaining ingredients in order given. Shape into small balls. If you wish, roll in sesame seed until lightly coated. Make an indentation in the center. Bake on greased cookie sheet for fifteen minutes at 375 degrees or until lightly browned. Cool and fill indentation with apricot jam. Yield: about four dozen.

Abbie's Hermit Cookies

No cookie jar is complete without hermits.

¼ cup margarine or butter	¼ teaspoon cinnamon
¾ cup brown sugar	¼ teaspoon allspice
1 egg	¾ cup chopped dates
1 cup brown rice flour	¾ cup raisins
2 tablespoons soya flour	1½ tablespoons milk
½ teaspoon salt	½ teaspoon rum flavoring
1 teaspoon soda	

Cream butter and sugar, add egg and beat until light and fluffy. Sift dry ingredients together and add to creamed mix, add milk and flavoring and beat until thoroughly blended. Fold in dates and raisins. Drop by teaspoonsful onto well-greased cookie tin and bake at 400 degrees for about ten minutes. Yield: approximately three dozen.

Note: If you have currants, add these to your batter, along with the dates and raisins, adjusting the amounts accordingly.

Meringues

Almost a confection!

2 egg whites	2 teaspoons baking powder
⅔ cup sugar	1 teaspoon vanilla

Beat egg whites until foamy, sift sugar and baking powder together and add one tablespoon at a time, beating until the sugar has been dissolved. Do not skimp on the beating—a secret of a good meringue. Cover cookie sheets with plain paper, ungreased. Bake at 275 degrees for forty-five to sixty minutes or until delicately browned and dry on surface. Remove from paper while warm. Yield: about five to six dozen.

Additions:

Take your choice:

1. One package semi-sweet chocolate chips (small).
2. Mix two tablespoons Dutch cocoa with sugar.
3. Fold in one cup chopped dates.
4. If you eat nuts, fold in one cup of the nuts of your choice.

5. Crush center of meringue after it is baked and fill with crushed strawberries, then top with whipped cream.

6. Fill center with jam of your choice.

7. If you use fruit, you may like to add one teaspoon lemon juice.

Section 6

DESSERTS—JOY TO THE SWEET TOOTH

Ice Creams and Sherbets

For our dieters, commercial ice creams and sherbets are banned. Join us for taste treats found in the homemade "Gourmet" ices.

Mary Ellen's Ice Cream

Everyone is making Mary Ellen's ice cream.

2 cups Eagle Brand condensed   2 quarts half and half cream
  milk
2 tablespoons vanilla

Fill freezer can with milk to within one-fourth of the top. Freeze. Yield: one gallon.

Lemon Sherbet

¾ cup sugar   ½ cup lemon juice
Pinch of salt   2 egg whites, stiffly beaten
1 cup water   ¼ cup sugar
½ cup top milk or light cream

Combine sugar, salt and water; cook five minutes. Cool. Add milk and then, very gradually, lemon juice. Freeze firm. Just before taking base from freezer beat egg whites until they hold their shape, and very gradually add one-fourth cup sugar and beat until stiff. Break frozen mixture into chunks and turn into chilled bowl. Beat fluffy smooth, fold in beaten egg whites and return quickly to freezer. Freeze firm. The recipe serves six.

Tangerine—Yogurt Sherbet

Tangy and refreshing.

Blend 1 cup yogurt with
⅓ cup sugar
1 6-ounce can tangerine
  juice

Juice and peel of 1 lemon
2 egg whites, stiffly
  beaten

Freeze in ice tray until mixture is firm but not solid, about two hours. Beat until smooth and fluffy. Fold in the stiffly beaten egg whites; return to ice tray and freeze until firm. Yield: one quart.

Cranberry Frappe

Tucson Marion's Christmas glamour!

1½ teaspoons gelatin
½ cup cold water
1 pint cranberries

1½ cups boiling water
1¼ cup sugar
2 tablespoons lemon juice

Soften gelatin in cold water, and combine with cranberries which have been cooked in boiling water until tender, then pressed through a fine sieve or cheese cloth.

Add sugar and lemon juice, stir until sugar is dissolved, chill and freeze. Remove from pan to mixing bowl and beat at high speed until light and smooth. Return to freezer and freeze until firm. Yield: serves six.

Frozen Lemon Cream

½ cup sugar
2 well-beaten eggs
½ cup light Karo

1 cup milk
¼ cup lemon juice
1 cup whipping cream

Gradually add sugar to eggs, beat until light and lemon-colored; add Karo, Milk, and lemon juice and mix thoroughly. Freeze firm in freezer tray. Break into chunks and beat until fluffy smooth. Fold in whipped cream and return quickly to the freezer; freeze firm. Serves six.

Chocolate Surprise

Chocolate fudge ice cream with a crunchy surprise inside.

3 squares semi-sweet chocolate	4 cups Rice Krinkles crushed to 1½ cups
½ cup sugar	¼ cup brown sugar
¼ cup orange juice	½ teaspoon grated orange peel, ¼ teaspoon for each part
¼ cup water	3 tablespoons melted butter
3 eggs, separated	½ teaspoon Cream of Tartar
1 cup whipping cream	¾ cup confectioner's sugar

Melt the chocolate in a double boiler. Add sugar, orange, and water. Heat. Beat the egg yolks, beat a small amount of chocolate mixture into the egg yolks, and then beat into the remaining chocolate mixture. Heat, stirring constantly until thickened. Cool. Fold in whipped cream. Combine rice crumbs, brown sugar, one-fourth teaspoon orange peel, and butter. Spread two-thirds of the crumbs evenly in bottom of a buttered pan, 13 x 9 x 2 inches, if you have it. If not, approximate it. Beat egg whites and Cream of Tartar until foamy. Beat in confectioner's sugar gradually until stiff peaks form. Add one-fourth teaspoon orange peel. Mix well. Spoon meringue onto crumbs. Pour chocolate sauce on top. Cut through mixture several times to give marbled look. Spread evenly on the pan. Top with the remaining crumbs. Freeze three to four hours. Yield: fifteen to eighteen servings.

Note: You may use bitter chocolate for stronger flavor, or an equal amount of carob bar.

Peppermint Ice Cream

Very easy to make and so refreshing to eat! Especially delicious served with chocolate brownies.

3 Rennet tablets	1½ cups sugar
3 tablespoons cold water	1¼ teaspoons Essence of Peppermint
6 cups top milk or half and half	Few drops of green coloring

Crush Rennet tablets in cold water, dissolve; combine top milk and sugar; heat slowly until comfortably warm when tested by dropping a few drops on your arm. Add green coloring and peppermint; add dissolved Rennet tablets, stirring only until it is completely blended. Let stand at room temperature *without* moving until set. Pour into ice cream freezer and freeze.

Note: This may be made as rich as you wish. If you want to use heavy cream for part of the cream, add it just as it is poured into ice cream freezer, unwhipped.

Refrigerator Mint Ice Cream

2 Rennet tablets dissolved in 2 tablespoons cold water	1 cup cream, whipped
	Few drops green coloring
3 cups milk	½ teaspoon Essence of Peppermint
1 cup sugar	

Combine milk and sugar and heat slowly until comfortably warm to finger. Add dissolved Rennet tablets. Tint a delicate green. Allow to set undisturbed until thick. Place in ice cube trays and freeze until firm. Break into chunks; turn into a chilled bowl and beat until fluffy smooth. Quickly beat in whipped cream. Return to freezer and freeze until desired firmness.

Note: Salt may be added to mixture if desired; one-fourth teaspoon for the small amount above, one-half teaspoon for the larger amount. Be sure you use Essence of Peppermint, which is usually obtained at a drug store.

Chocolate Mint Roll

Who says you must live a dull life, gastronomically speaking, when on a diet? This is gourmet food for anyone.

5 eggs	¼ teaspoon soda
¾ cup sugar	2 1-ounce squares bitter chocolate
1 tablespoon potato flour plus enough brown rice flour to fill ½ cup measure	2 tablespoons sugar
¼ teaspoon salt	3 tablespoons cold water
1 teaspoon baking powder	1 teaspoon vanilla

Beat eggs and three-fourths cup sugar until thick and light. Add sifted dry ingredients all at once. Fold lightly until blended. Have ready-melted chocolate which has been combined with two tablespoons of sugar and three table-spoons cold water, then add vanilla. Fold quickly into batter, blending well. Pour into a 9 x 14 inch pan which has been lined with greased wax paper. Bake at 375 degrees for fifteen to eighteen minutes. Turn cake out onto clean towel sprinkled with more sugar; peel off paper. Roll up cake, wrap in towel and cool. When cool, very carefully unroll and spread with Mint Ice Cream (see Dessert Section). Reroll, bringing towel up around cake as if to hold it. Freeze. Just before serving, frost with chocolate frosting or whipped cream.

Note: You make this into a loaf by cutting the sheet into four sections. Spread with ice cream as for layer cake and frost as desired.

French Custard

A great favorite, smoother and richer than regular custard with crunchy topping.

2 cups light (half-and-half) cream	½ teaspoon salt
	1 teaspoon vanilla
4 egg yolks	2 tablespoons brown
2½ tablespoons sugar	sugar

Heat cream until a film puckers over the top. Remove from heat at once. Beat yolks until light in color and thick, gradually beating in sugar and salt. Pour a little of the scalded cream into egg mixture and stir vigorously. Pour in remainder in the same manner, stirring constantly. Add the vanilla. Pour into a one-quart baking dish, place the dish in a pan of hot water and bake one hour at 350 degrees or until a silver knife comes out clean when tested in the center of the custard. Cool, then sift brown sugar over the entire top, slide dish under the broiler four to five inches from the flame. Broil until the sugar melts and turns slightly

. hard and crunchy. Watch it closely to prevent burning. Cool in refrigerator. Serves four.

Note: Be sure to cool custard before putting under broiler, otherwise it will continue to cook and will be spoiled.

Plain Custard

2 cups milk	¼ teaspoon salt
2 whole eggs or 4 egg yolks	1 teaspoon vanilla
⅓ cup sugar	¼ teaspoon nutmeg

Scald milk, add very gradually, starting with a very little, to the eggs which have been beaten with sugar, salt, and vanilla. When blended sprinkle nutmeg over the top. Bake in a Pyrex or pottery bowl set in a pan of water for one hour at 350 degrees or until a silver knife comes out clean when inserted in the center of the custard. Serves four.

Hot Fruit Medley

For people who cannot eat fresh fruit.

1 orange	1 cup canned apricots
1 lemon	1 cup canned sliced peaches
½ cup brown sugar	1 cup pineapple tidbits
¼ teaspoon nutmeg	2 cups pitted Bing cherries

Grate the rind from the orange and lemon; add brown sugar with nutmeg. Cut the orange and lemon in very thin slices; butter one-quart casserole. Arrange well-drained fruit in layers, sprinkling each layer with brown sugar and nutmeg mixture. Bake thirty minutes. Serve warm with a spoonful of sour cream. Serves six to eight.

Lemon Chiffon Ring With Fresh Fruit

Garnish with frosted green grapes for extra glamour.

4 teaspoons gelatin	½ cup cold water

⅔ cup sugar	2 teaspoons grated lemon
⅔ cup lemon juice	rind
6 eggs	⅓ cup sugar
¼ teaspoon salt	

Soften gelatin in water and let stand a few minutes. Mix two-thirds cup sugar with lemon juice. Separate eggs and beat yolks and salt until quite thick and lemon-yellow. Add the lemon juice and sugar to egg yolks, stirring constantly. Cook in the top of a double boiler until the mixture forms a thin coating on the spoon. Remove from heat, add gelatin and stir until dissolved. Add lemon rind and chill until it begins to thicken. Beat egg whites until they stand in peaks. Add one-third cup sugar, one tablespoon at a time, beating well after each addition. Fold in gelatin mixture, pour into a large-ring mold and chill until set. Unmold and fill center with seedless green grapes and fresh strawberries. If desired, you may top ring with whipped cream to which chopped mint has been added.

Note: Fresh peaches or cantaloupe are delicious as a substitute for strawberries.

Clara's Lemon Chiffon Pudding

Quick, easy, delicious, and complete with its own sauce.

¾ cup sugar	¼ cup lemon juice
2 tablespoons brown rice flour	1 cup milk
2 tablespoons soft butter	3 egg whites (beaten)
3 egg yolks	

In your mixer blend sugar, flour, butter, egg yolks, and lemon juice until smooth and thoroughly blended; slowly add the milk; fold in the beaten egg whites, and with a wire whip, cut through the egg yolk batter until the egg whites are completely incorporated into it. Pour into a shallow unbuttered baking dish, set into a pan of hot water and bake at 350 degrees for about forty minutes. Serves four.

Note: You may use orange or pineapple juice for a

taste change if you wish.

Date Tarts

3 eggs, separated	1 tablespoon potato flour
¾ cup sugar	1 teaspoon baking powder
1 pound dates (2 cups)	½ cup sesame seed,
2 tablespoons rice polish	toasted

Beat egg yolks until very light. Add sugar and blend thoroughly. Cut dates into quite fine pieces. Sift rice polish, potato flour, and baking powder together, and then sift again over the dates. Sprinkle sesame seed over the mixture. Fold in the well-beaten whites of the eggs. Bake in paper-lined muffin tins in 350-degree oven for fifteen to twenty minutes. Serve warm or cool with whipped cream. Makes two dozen tarts.

Dorothy's Marshmallow Crunch Cups

¼ pound marshmallows	3 cups Rice Krinkles
2 tablespoons butter	

Place marshmallows and butter in top of double boiler. When a syrup is formed, pour it over the Rice Krinkles which you have ready in a buttered bowl. Mix thoroughly and make into shells by packing into custard cups about 3¾ inches across. Make fairly thin shells. Let set until firm, then fill with ice cream. Serves six.

Fluffy Fig Pudding

A substitute for plum pudding at Christmas.

1 pound dried figs	1 teaspoon cinnamon
1¾ cups milk	¾ teaspoon salt
1½ cups brown rice flour	5 eggs
2½ teaspoons baking powder	1¼ cups ground suet
1 cup sugar	1½ cups rice waffle crumbs
1 teaspoon nutmeg	3 tablespoons grated orange rind

Several days ahead, snip the stems from the figs with

scissors. Then snip the figs into small pieces, add milk and cook over boiling water twenty minutes. Sift together the flour, baking powder, sugar, nutmeg, cinnamon, and salt. In a bowl, beat eggs and add the remainder of ingredients. Mix well and turn into well-greased two-quart mold or smaller molds of your size choice. Fill no more than two-thirds full. Cover tightly and place on trivet in deep kettle. Add enough boiling water to come halfway up the sides of the mold. Steam for two hours. Let stand two minutes. Remove from mold. Serve hot with sauce.

Party Glamour

Make meringue shell.

4 egg yolks	3 tablespoons lemon juice
½ cup sugar	1 tablespoon grated lemon
1 cup milk	rind
1 envelope plain gelatin	⅛ teaspoon salt
	½ pint heavy cream

Beat egg yolks in double boiler top; stir in one-half cup sugar and one-half cup milk. Cook over boiling water until thick. Add geltain which has been softened in one-half cup milk to the hot mixture. Stir until gelatin has completely melted. Remove from heat and add lemon; cool. When mixture is cool and just starting to set, fold in whipped cream and salt. Pour into meringue shell. Chill from twelve to twenty-four hours. To serve, garnish with whipped cream and sprinkle with coconut which has been toasted. You may top with fresh or frozen fruit such as strawberries or peaches if you wish.

Pink Velvet

This is beautiful to look at as well as being luscious to eat.

2 Rennet tablets	2 tablespoons of cold water

Dissolve the Rennet tablets in two tablespoons of cold

water.

1½ cups milk	2 boxes frozen raspberries
½ cup sugar	2 cups whipping cream
¼ teaspoon salt	1 teaspoon vanilla

Heat the milk, sugar, and salt until comfortably warm to your finger. Remove from the heat, pour into a dish for freezing, quickly add the Rennet and stir until blended, allow to set undisturbed until it has thickened. Place in freezer and freeze firm. When frozen, cut into squares and whip in your electric mixer until smooth and fluffy. Have ready to fold into this the raspberries which have been mixed in your blender and strained to remove the seeds and the cream which has been whipped and flavored. Refreeze until firm. This will serve six to eight people. You may wish to have this sweeter, but take into consideration that the raspberries are already sweetened.

Grasshopper

2 envelopes unflavored gelatin	6 eggs, separated
1 cup cold water	½ cup green creme de menthe
1 cup sugar	½ cup white creme de cacao
¼ teaspoon salt	1 pint heavy cream

Sprinkle gelatin over water in a medium saucepan. Add one-half cup sugar, salt, and egg yolks; stir until thoroughly blended. Place over low heat; stir constantly until gelatin dissolves and mixture thickens slightly. Remove from heat; Stir in creme de menthe and creme de cacao. Chill, stirring frequently until mixture starts to hold its shape. Meanwhile, beat egg whites in large bowl until stiff but not dry. Gradually add remaining one-half cup sugar and beat until very stiff. Fold in gelatin mixture. Fold in whipped cream. Turn into mold or molds. Chill until firm. Garnish with whipped cream and sprinkle with grated chocolate.

Note: You may fill chocolate pie crust with this for a delicious pie.

Cream Puffs, Eclairs or Fritters

Versatile, adaptable, and so easy to make

1 cup water	1 cup unsifted rice flour
½ cup *butter*	plus 1 tablespoon
¼ teaspoon salt	5 eggs
1 teaspoon sugar	

Heat water, butter, salt, and sugar until butter is melted; bring to a full rolling boil. Add flour which you have sifted after measuring all at once; remove from heat and continue stirring vigorously until mixture is smooth and thick, leaving sides of the pan to follow the spoon. Add eggs, one at a time, beating smooth after each addition until dough is smooth and satiny, and the beater breaks dough when lifted. Cool for fifteen minutes before shaping.

Drop about three tablespoons of dough onto a greased baking sheet, spacing puffs about three inches apart. Bake in 400-degree oven for thirty-five minutes to forty-five minutes, or until puffs are golden and lightweight. Split while hot to allow steam to escape. To fill this recipe of puffs, you will need six cups of whipped cream, ice cream, or pastry cream. Yield: approximately twenty puffs.

Peppermint Cream Filling for Cream Puffs

Luscious when cream puff is topped with chocolate sauce!

Break one-half pound peppermint stick candy into small pieces; melt in one-half cup water by keeping the water hot but not boiling; add one cup evaporated milk, bring back to boiling point, add one envelope of gelatin which has been softened in two tablespoons of cold water. Chill until partially set. Whip one-half pint of cream until it holds its shape well, then fold into peppermint mixture. Fill cream puff shells. If desired, top with chocolate sauce.

French Pastry Cream

¾ cup sugar	4 egg yolks or 2 eggs
½ cup brown rice flour	2 cups milk, scalded
¼ teaspoon salt	1 teaspoon vanilla

Combine dry ingredients and mix with slightly beaten egg yolks; stir in enough hot milk to make a thin paste. Add paste to remaining hot milk and cook over boiling water five minutes, stirring constantly; cook ten minutes longer, or until mixture is thickened, stirring occasionally. Cool and add vanilla. For a richer filling, cool and then fold in one-half cup of cream, whipped until quite stiff.

Croquembouche

Bake tiny puffs, or at least ones much smaller than the regular puffs. For this, use one to two tablespoons of dough each. Bake thirty to thirty-five minutes in 400-degree oven. Fill with pastry cream and place in refrigerator until ready to mold.

Mold

Make a cone from a piece of lightweight cardboard 18 x 24 inches. Cover the cardboard with wax paper or foil. Fasten cone to hold shape and set it into an empty two-quart milk carton. Butter well inside of cone with soft butter. With a long fork, dip the top of the cream in carmelized sugar and center it at the bottom of the cone. Repeat, dipping one puff at a time and placing it on top of the puffs, until you reach the top of your cone, building a hollow wall inside of the cone. When the top is reached, arrange the puffs to make an even edge (this will be the bottom of your croquembouche on which it will rest).

Place in the refrigerator until you are ready to serve. Unwrap and place on the serving tray. To serve, break off individual puffs with a fork. Yield: sixteen to eighteen servings.

Use caramel syrup for Croquembouche. If the caramel thickens while making croquembouche, place the pan over hot water.

Eclairs

Make each eclair about four inches long, using about the same amount of dough as used for the puff, and place two to three inches apart on a greased baking sheet. Proceed as for cream puffs. You will need the same amount of filling.

To frost: a 14-ounce bar of melted sweet-milk chocolate makes a quick and delicious topping. Also most delicious when topped with honey just as it is served.

Fritters

Decrease the butter to one-third cup. Drop by rounded teaspoon into salad oil which has been heated to 370 degrees. Fry until golden brown or until they stop turning. Roll in sugar and serve hot, or serve topped with honey at once.

Petite Puffs

Use one tablespoon paste for each puff. Place two inches apart on greased baking sheet. Bake at 400 degrees for about twenty-five minutes or until puffs are golden and lightweight. Wonderful for cocktail appetizers when filled with fish, chicken, or meat.

Quick and Easy Filling

Make up a recipe of prepared vanilla pudding which lists cornstarch as the thickener, fold in one cup of whipped cream. Flavor to your taste.

Cream Filling

Very delicious in a real cream puff!

4 teaspoons gelatin	6 tablespoons sugar
1½ cups rich milk	6 tablespoons rice flour
2 whole eggs	1 teaspoon salt
2 egg yolks	

Soften gelatin in one-fourth cup milk; mix one and one-fourth cups of the milk with eggs, sugar, flour, and salt. Stir over heat until just to the point of boiling. Remove and stir over ice until cold. Add:

2 egg whites, stiffly beaten	2 tablespoons rum or
2 cups cream, whipped	2 teaspoons vanilla

You may drip caramel syrup or chocolate syrup over the filled puffs.

Caramel Syrup

2 cups sugar	½ teaspoon Cream of Tartar
1½ cups water	

Place in a heavy pan, bring slowly to a boil and cook very slowly until syrup starts to turn caramel. Remove at once from heat and place in a bowl of water to keep the syrup from cooking further. Pour spoon of syrup over each puff. This can burn quickly, so watch it!

Chocolate Syrup

¼ cup corn syrup	1 square bitter chocolate
½ cup sugar	½ teaspoon vanilla
½ cup water	

Cook to soft ball stage, remove from heat and add one square of chocolate. Stir until it melts and add one-half teaspoon vanilla. May be thinned by adding cream if it becomes too stiff.

Carol's Fudge Sauce

Carol calls this everybody's "special." For more than thirty years my sister-in-law has been sharing this recipe with her family and friends. It is the best fudge sauce I have ever eaten.

4 squares unsweetened chocolate	½ pint heavy cream
	1 can condensed milk
3 tablespoons butter	1 teaspoon vanilla
1½ cups sugar	

Melt the chocolate and butter in the double boiler, add the sugar and cream and, when heated, cook for five minutes, then add condensed milk and vanilla. Cook to the desired thickness. This may be thinned with milk. It will keep for a very long time in the refrigerator. One-half of this amount is enough for eight servings over ice cream or puddings.

Section 7

PASTRY AND PIES–LET'S BE SPECIAL

Pastry, like bread, will be different. My early attempts at making pastry were enough to make any cook sit down and howl! Since flour without gluten makes a crust with "no stretch strength," and with a texture on the tongue much like fine, fine sand, something has to be added to improve the texture and to supply some measure of togetherness. The use of egg, potato flour, and/or cheese help achieve this. The two recipes given below provide very palatable crusts. When a wheat-eater asks for a second piece of pie and raves about the crust, you know that you have made the grade!

Gather together all your patience and determination. Roll the crust between sheets of floured wax paper or foil. If you use foil you may leave it under the bottom crust as a pie plate or pie plate liner. When the dough is thin enough, gently detach the top paper, but leave it over the crust, flip the crust sandwiched between the papers, and detach the lower paper. Remove the top side paper and lay the crust over your rolling pin; very gently lower this onto the pie plate. Smooth it out and repair any broken pieces. This crust does not become hard or tough from extra working if this becomes necessary. Roll out top crust in like manner, but after crust is detached from paper, remove top paper and very smoothly flip crust over the top of the pie by use of bottom paper. If you are lucky, there will be no breaks.

I have not included recipes for berry or fruit pies other than the very special rhubarb pie. The procedure for these pies is the same as any regular recipe. You may use rice flour, cornstarch, or tapioca for thickening.

75

Although the foregoing instructions sound involved, it is not too difficult. It really depends upon how much you want that piece of pie!

Pastry

A good basic crust. Makes one double crust pie.

¼ teaspoon Cream of Tartar	½ cup shortening
1½ cups brown rice flour	1 egg
3 tablespoons potato flour	⅓ cup plus 1 tablespoon milk
½ teaspoon salt	

Sift the dry ingredients together; cut in shortening; add egg and milk and stir into a ball. Knead a few seconds. Roll out between sheets of wax paper or foil. Brush the top crust with a slightly beaten egg white and sprinkle with sugar. This gives a golden brown, very pretty crust; you can also brush the top of the crust with milk and sprinkle with sugar. If you fail to do either, your crust will be quite pallid. Bake at 425 degrees ten to twelve minutes for single crust. You will find this is a crisper crust than one made with wheat flour.

Note: Try adding one-fourth cup mashed potato to your pie dough. It makes a softer but easier to handle dough.

Cream Cheese Crust

Flaky and delicious for double crust pies.

½ cup margarine or butter	⅛ teaspoon baking powder
1 cup brown rice flour	1 3-ounce package cream cheese
¼ teaspoon salt	
1 tablespoon potato flour	1 whole egg

Cut the margarine into the sifted dry ingredients. Cut in the cream cheese, and add egg which has been beaten. Knead into a ball and roll out in the usual manner. Brush the top crust with a slightly beaten egg white and sprinkle with sugar. Makes one double or two single crust pies. Bake at 425 degrees for ten to twelve minutes for single crust.

Chocolate-Coconut Pie Shell

2 ounces unsweetened
  chocolate
2 tablespoons butter
2 tablespoons hot milk

⅔ cup confectioner's sugar
1½ cups finely chopped
  flaked coconut

Melt together the chocolate and butter over boiling water. Mix milk with the sugar and add the chocolate. Stir well. Put in the coconut and mix. Spread on bottom and sides of pie plate. Chill until firm. Yield: one 8-inch pie.

Coconut Pie Shell

2 cans Angel Flake coconut   5 tablespoons butter

Melt butter in a large skillet. Add coconut and stir constantly until golden brown. Remove from skillet to a 9-inch pie plate to prevent continued browning. Press coconut against bottom and sides of the pie plate. Avoid getting too much concentrated on the bottom.

Rice Krinkle Crust

This can be used for an ice cream pie or a filling that is going to be served at once.

¼ cup butter or margarine   3 cups Rice Krinkles
1 cup brown sugar

Melt the butter and brown sugar in a heavy pan. When the sugar is dissolved and the mixture bubbles, slowly pour the syrup over the Rice Krinkles which have been placed in a greased mixing bowl. Toss with a fork as you pour, working quickly. Press into 9-inch pie plate. Chill.

Creme de Menthe Pie

A joy to the taste buds.

1 tablespoon gelatin
½ cup cold milk
1½ cups milk, scalded
¾ cup sugar

1 tablespoon cornstarch
3 eggs, separated
2 teaspoons water

Soften gelatin in one-half cup cold milk. Scald milk in double boiler. Combine sugar, cornstarch, egg yolks, and water, and stir until smooth. Add to the milk in the double boiler and cook until custard coats the spoon. Add gelatin and chill until thickened.

Melt two squares of bitter chocolate and cool. Beat chilled custard until smooth and add:

    3 stiffly-beaten egg whites   ½ cup whipped cream.

Divide this mixture in half. To one-half, add melted chocolate. To the other, add one-fourth cup creme de menthe. Add a few drops of green coloring.

Put minted custard in the baked pie shell and let it stand in the refrigerator until partially set. Then, and only then, put the chocolate portion on top of the mint portion. Chill several hours and top with whipped cream garnish.

Super Rhubarb Cream Pie

Use pink rhubarb and wait for the rave notices!

1½ cups sugar	2 well beaten eggs
3 tablespoons rice flour	3 cups cut rhubarb (cut
½ teaspoon nutmeg	not more than 1-inch
1 tablespoon butter	squares
	1 recipe plain pastry

Blend sugar, flour, nutmeg, and butter; add eggs, beat smooth. Pour over rhubarb in 9-inch pastry lined pie pan. Top with pastry. Brush pastry with slightly beaten egg white and sprinkle with sugar. Bake in hot oven 450 degrees for ten minutes, reduce heat to 350 degrees and bake for thirty minutes longer. In using rice flour pastry, I find that it is best to wrap the edges in pastry paper. A two-inch strip cut from a man's jersey undershirt makes an excellent pastry edging!—a good use for them when runs have taken over their first life.

Lemon Chiffon Pie

Delicious!

4 eggs, separated
½ cup lemon juice
½ teaspoon salt
¾ cup sugar

1 tablespoon unflavored
  gelatin softened in
  ¼ cup cold water
1 teaspoon grated lemon
  rind

Beat egg yolks and put in top of double boiler with lemon juice, salt, and one-fourth cup sugar. Cook over hot water until custard consistency, then add gelatin which has been soaking in cold water. When gelatin has dissolved, stir in lemon rind. Cool. When mixture begins to thicken, fold in egg whites which have been stiffly beaten with the remaining one-half cup sugar. Fill a baked 9-inch pie shell and chill in the refrigerator. Sweetened cream makes a delicious topping for this pie—whip and barely sweeten, as your pie is sweet enough.

Frozen Eggnog Pie

Super for Christmas or any old time.

1⅓ cups sesame seed
    cookie crumbs
¼ cup sugar

¼ teaspoon nutmeg
¼ teaspoon cinnamon
¼ cup butter or margarine

Roll cookies with a rolling pin until fine crumbs. A plastic bag works very well for rolling crumbs. Combine with sugar, nutmeg, and cinnamon. Butter bottom and sides of a 10-inch pie plate thoroughly. Shake mixture over the bottom and sides of pie plate allowing the butter to catch the crumbs. Bake for five minutes, only to set, at 300 degrees.

Filling

2 eggs
⅔ cup sugar
⅛ teaspoon salt
1 envelope unflavored
  gelatin

⅓ cup rum or Creme de cacao
1 teaspoon rum flavoring
2 cups heavy cream, whipped
½ cup sifted confectioner's
  sugar

Beat eggs with sugar and salt at high speed until well

combined and fluffy. Set bowl in pan of hot water and continue beating at high speed until mixture begins to thicken, in three to five minutes. Sprinkle gelatin over liquor in small bowl, let stand about five minutes to soften. Add rum flavoring. Beat gelatin mixture into egg mixture and combine thoroughly to dissolve gelatin. Remove from hot water and let cool, stirring frequently. In a large bowl, beat cream with confectioner's sugar until it holds its shape. Gently fold in cooled egg mixture until well combined. Turn into a prepared pie shell. Sprinkle top with nutmeg. Freeze until firm for four to five hours. This is also delicious unfrozen.

Jane's Cherry Cream Pie

Jane makes unusual desserts and this is one of them. I use sesame seed cookies as a substitute for graham crackers.

Crust

Sesame Seed cookie crumbs to make one and one-half cups. One-half cup of butter rubbed liberally over pan to make bed for crumbs. Press crumbs into pan and refrigerate.

Filling. Mix with beater.

3 small cream cheese (3 ounces)	2 eggs, beaten
½ cup sugar	1 teaspoon vanilla
	1 small carton sour cream

Pour into pie shell and bake at 375 degrees for twenty-five minutes. Cool.

Topping

Pour off liquid of one small can Supreme sour red cherries. Cook liquid with three-fourths cup sugar. Add a squeeze of lemon juice, and bring to a boil. Make a paste of three and one-half tablespoons cornstarch and three tablespoons water and add to juice. Cook until thick. Add teaspoon red food color, fold in cherries, and pour over pie.

Makes one 9-inch pie.

Note: You may use a slightly underbaked pie crust shell.

Mocha Chiffon Pie

9-inch pastry crust or
  coconut crust

2 envelopes unflavored
  gelatin

½ cup water

1 cup hot coffee (you may
  use 1½ teaspoons instant
  coffee with 1 cup hot
  water if you wish)

½ ounce chocolate

⅓ cup sugar

½ cup evaporated milk

2 egg yolks

1 teaspoon vanilla

1 cup whipping cream

¼ cup sugar

2 stiffly beaten egg whites

¼ teaspoon salt

Soften the gelatin in cold water, add the hot coffee, and stir until gelatin is dissolved. Add the chocolate and after it is melted, add one-third cup sugar and one-half cup evaporated milk. Pour mixture on the egg yolks which have been well beaten. Cook in double boiler until thickened. Cool, add vanilla, and when almost ready to set, beat until light and fluffy. Be careful that you do not let it set or you will have lumps. Whip the one cup of cream, beat egg whites and salt until stiff but not dry, add remaining sugar gradually. Fold whipped cream into coffee mixture and last fold in the egg whites. Pour into crust and chill until set. Top with whipped cream and garnish with shaved chocolate. Yield: six servings. This is rich enough to cut into eight servings.

Krinkle Crunch Pie

1 cup chocolate niblets or
  6 ounces semi-sweet
  chocolate

3 tablespoons butter

2 cups Rice Krinkles, lightly
  crushed

1 quart Mint Ice Cream

1 ounce bitter chocolate,
  shaved

In the top of the double boiler, combine chocolate niblets and butter, melt and blend. Add Rice Krinkles and mix well. Press into unbuttered 9-inch pie plate; chill until firm. Fill layers of ice cream into crust, topped with shaved bitter chocolate. Serves six. Or:

Make individual Krinkle cups, place a scoop of ice cream in each and top with shaved chocolate.

Peppermint Chiffon Pie

The taste of a peppermint sundae with chocolate sauce.

Chocolate coconut crust	½ cup sugar
1 tablespoon unflavored gelatin	1 cup cream
	1 teaspoon vanilla
¼ cup cold water	1 cup crushed peppermint stick candy
3 egg whites	
	½ teaspoon mint flavoring

Soften gelatin in cold water and dissolve over hot water. Beat egg whites until stiff and beat in sugar gradually. Add dissolved gelatin to egg whites and fold in whipped cream, flavoring, and crushed candy. Pour into chocolate coconut crust. Just before serving garnish with whipped cream and sprinkle with crushed candy.

Grandmother's Pumpkin Pie

A slightly different seasoning.

1 small can pumpkin or 2 cups home prepared pumpkin	1 scant teaspoon ginger (about ¾ teaspoon)
1 scant cup sugar	½ teaspoon nutmeg
½ teaspoon salt	2 eggs
1 teaspoon cinnamon	1½ cups milk

Put pumpkin, sugar, salt, seasoning, and eggs into mixing bowl. Beat until smooth. Add milk gradually, beating all the while. Pour into pastry crust. Bake fifteen minutes at 400 degrees, then reduce heat to 350 degrees and cook from forty-five to sixty minutes. When the knife inserted into the center of pie comes away clean, the pie is done. Do not overcook. With a rice crust, it is better to put a paper or cloth shield over the edge of the crust. Otherwise it browns too much.

Lemon Meringue Pie

Tart lemon, sweet crisp meringue. Nectar!

4 egg yolks	½ cup lemon juice
⅔ cup sugar	1 envelope unflavored gelatin
2 teaspoons grated lemon peel	1 cup water, using ¼ cup for softening gelatin

Beat egg yolks until thick and lemon colored. Gradually add two-thirds cup sugar. Beat in grated lemon peel and lemon juice. Cook in double boiler until thickened—about five minutes. Add softened gelatin and three-fourths cup hot water. Cool. When thickened, fold in one cup heavy cream, whipped, to which two tablespoons sugar has been added while beating.

Sue's Meringue

The first meringue I found dependable.

4 egg whites	4 teaspoons baking powder
1⅓ cups sugar	

Beat egg whites until foamy. Add very gradually, one tablespoon at a time, the sugar to which the baking powder has been added and sifted. Continue beating until the sugar has dissolved. This takes a long time. Small additions of sugar with plenty of beatings between are the secret of a perfect meringue. Beat until very stiff and glossy. Spread on well-greased, well-floured pie plate. Use extra mixture to make individual meringues as this pie will not need the entire amount. Bake at 275 degrees for one and one-fourth hours. Cool before covering with lemon mixture. Garnish with whipped cream if you wish.

Section 8

MAIN DISHES—SPECIALTIES OF THE HOUSE

Scalloped Oysters

We always like to have scalloped oysters on Christmas Eve, a tradition of ours, and it is nice to make them especially "gourmet" food for this occasion.

1 pint oysters	¼ teaspoon grated lemon rind
3 tablespoons butter	Dash of nutmeg
3 tablespoons brown rice flour	Salt and pepper
	2 cups waffle croutons
1 cup cream	⅓ cup grated Parmesan cheese
⅓ cup dry Sherry	
1 teaspoon lemon juice	Dash of paprika

Drain oysters, saving the liquid; melt butter, and stir in rice flour until smooth. Add cream and cook, stirring until mixture boils and thickens. Add wine, lemon juice and rind, nutmeg, oyster liquid, and salt and pepper. Arrange half of the oysters in a greased casserole, then half of the croutons and half of the sauce. Repeat until all ingredients are used. Sprinkle cheese over the top, dust with paprika, and bake at 450 degrees for about twenty-five minutes. Serves four.

To prepare croutons: cut a Brown Rice Polish Waffle into one-half inch cubes, place on cookie sheet and brush with butter. Bake at 325 degrees for fifteen to twenty minutes until dry and crisp. Stir occasionally to brown evenly.

Oyster Rarebit

Some people like Rarebit for Sunday supper like

84

"Chicken Every Sunday." This one is party fare whether there is a party or not!

2 tablespoons butter	3 cups grated cheddar
2 tablespoons rice flour	cheese
1 cup milk	Few grains cayenne pepper
½ cup light cream or evaporated milk	2 slightly beaten eggs

In double boiler or chafing dish, melt butter and add flour stirring until velvety smooth, slowly add milk and cream, stirring until very smooth. Add grated cheese and cayenne pepper. When cheese is melted, stir a little of the sauce into the beaten eggs, stir smooth, add more and stir smooth again; turn heat *very low* to keep hot.

½ pound mushrooms	1 pint oysters

Saute the mushrooms in butter until golden brown. Remove from pan and add oysters in their liquid heating just until the edges curl. When ready to serve, add to the sauce given above and pour over rice polish baked waffles. Serves six.

Note: If you wish to be especially festive, fry bacon crisp and crumble small pieces into waffle mix and bake. Bake waffles and put in 325-degree oven for about ten minutes to increase crispness. The rice polish waffle is crisp and delicate, but this drying out adds a crunchiness which makes a pleasing contrast to the creamy rarebit.

Seafood Casserole

A delicious casserole which is topped with potato chips, another helper when wheat products are banned.

1 pound shrimp	1½ cups chopped celery
1 pound canned or frozen crab	¼ teaspoon salt
	Sprinkling of garlic salt
1 cup mayonnaise	¼ teaspoon basil
½ cup chopped green pepper	2 cups crushed potato chips
¼ cup chopped onion	Paprika

Thaw shrimp under running water and remove shells and clean; if crab should be fresh, prepare for cooking. Combine all ingredients excepting garlic, basil, and potato chips. Pour into a two and one-half quart casserole. Sprinkle with garlic salt and basil. Top with coarsely crushed potato chips, and sprinkle with paprika. Bake twenty-five minutes at 400 degrees. Yield: eight servings.

Note: If you can get scallops that are not breaded, you may substitute these for the crab. Of course, you may wash the breading off the scallops, but this is quite a waste.

Carol's Seafood Newberg

Flavor and elegance form a partnership when Carol entertains. This is a favorite of hers.

⅓ cup butter or margarine	1 cup cut-up cooked lobster
⅓ cup brown rice flour	1½ cups cut-up cooked
3 cups milk	scallops or shrimp
1½ tablespoons prepared mustard (mild)	2 cups cut-up cooked halibut or haddock
1½ teaspoons salt	1 cup cooked sliced mush-
¼ teaspoon paprika	rooms
¼ teaspoon pepper	⅓ cup grated cheese

Melt butter; add flour and blend; add seasonings and mix, then add fish. Put into one and one-half to two-quart casserole, sprinkle with cheese and bake for about twenty-five minutes at 350 degrees, or until sauce begins to bubble. Yield: eight to ten servings. This may be varied with many combinations.

Marian's Rolled Rump Roast With Herbs

This has been my favorite way to fix a beef roast since Marian first served it to us. The flavor is subtle and tantalizing.

Select the best six-pound rolled rump possible. Have on hand one-fourth pound of your choice of cheese—Swiss,

Mozarella, Cheddar, or Jack. Mix together:

1 teaspoon oregano	1 teaspoon meat tenderizer
1 teaspoon thyme	(without monosodium
1 teaspoon paprika	glutamate)

Cut the cheese into one-inch squares, one-fourth inch thick, and roll thoroughly in the mixed herbs. Slash the roast deeply about every two and one-half inches apart and push the cheese down into the slash. Roast in a covered roaster at 300 degrees for three and one-half hours. Allow about one-half pound meat per portion.

Apple-Stuffed Pork Chops

6 pork chops, 2 inches thick	1 large tart apple, peeled,
1 teaspoon salt	cored, and sliced thin
⅛ teaspoon pepper	½ teaspoon nutmeg
5 tablespoons chopped onion	¼ teaspoon cinnamon
3 tablespoons butter	2-3 tablespoons water
5 tablespoons seedless raisins	2 cups cooked rice

Have butcher prepare lean, meaty chops by making a pocket in the chop clear to the bone, but leaving all the meat along the bone attached. Pound thin with a mallet. Season with salt and pepper, using just one-half teaspoon of salt.

Saute onion in butter, add raisins, apple slices, remaining salt, nutmeg, cinnamon, and water; toss in the rice and mix with a tossing motion. Spread the dressing into the pork chops and fasten edges with skewers or toothpicks, or sew them. Put chops in shallow roasting pan; bake uncovered at 350 degrees for one and one-half hours. Turn once during baking and drain off any excess fat. You will not have much if you bought the suggested lean chops. Yield: six servings.

Syrian Lamb Stew

This recipe comes from Beirut. Esther's father was

a missionary doctor in Beirut for many years. We were brides, living in a small Vermont town when she gave me this recipe. In Syria, she told me, the cook browns the rice in oil and adds moisture very gradually as the rice swells and absorbs it. This takes a long time and I am my "cook," so I use a quick American way. Otherwise, there is no change from the original recipe.

3 pounds lamb shoulder	½ pound fresh string beans
1 large can tomatoes	or comparable amount of
6 large onions	frozen or canned string
6 carrots	beans
	Salt and pepper

Stew lamb until tender enough to remove the bones, or about two hours. Put tomatoes and onions into broth and cook until the onions are tender. This takes from thirty to sixty minutes, depending upon the onions. Add whole carrots, allowing twenty to thirty minutes for them to cook. The last ten minutes add the string beans. Serve over streamed rice unless you have time to make the "Stirred Rice."

Chicken Rosemary

Rosemary gives a delightful taste change to chicken.

Brown rice flour	½ onion of medium size
5 or 6 chicken breasts	6-inch branch of rosemary
½ cup melted butter or	(sprig)
margarine	6 tablespoons yogurt
Salt and pepper	

Roll breasts in brown rice flour and brown in melted butter. Place in baking dish and spread the sliced onion over the top. Break the rosemary sprig into three pieces and place over the top of the chicken. Daub one tablespoon yogurt on top of each breast. Sprinkle liberally with pepper; salt lightly. Bake two hours at 300 degrees. Yield: one serving per breast. Serve with rice.

*Note:*If fresh rosemary is not available, use the dried as you would pepper. Do not let your hand be too heavy on this as the dried is much stronger than the fresh.

Chicken Avocado Supreme

This has been a favorite dish at our house for many years, both for family and guests.

Chicken may be prepared the day before, if you wish.

2 three pound chickens	3 to 4 sprays of parsley
1 teaspoon salt	⅓ cup butter
Sprinkling of pepper	⅓ cup brown rice flour
Handful of celery leaves	2 egg yolks
2 stalks of celery	Avocado
1 large onion	1 cup almonds*

Wash chicken and put on to cook in a quart of water, or more if necessary. Add salt, pepper, celery, onion, and parsley. Cover and simmer until chicken is tender. Lift out chicken and cool; save the stock. Remove the skin and bones from chicken and put back into the chicken stock. Add one cup more water if necessary, and simmer slowly another hour. Strain stock. Melt one-third cup butter and one-third cup flour and mix until smooth. Add four cups of chicken stock and heat, stirring until the consistency of heavy cream. Then add the pieces of chicken and simmer until chicken is well-heated throughout. Beat the egg yolks slightly with one-fourth cup of the gravy. Heat slowly about five minutes, stirring constantly so that the egg yolks will not curdle. Season with salt and pepper. Just before serving add balls or slices cut from avocado. Serve over pimiento rice and sprinkle with toasted, slivered almonds.

Pimiento Rice

Cook five cups of rice until it is fluffy and dry. Add

---

*Almonds for your guests to eat, not for your dieter.

one can of drained pimiento and toss lightly. Arrange on a platter and serve covered with the chicken and sauce. Garnish with parsley.

Note: When removing the chicken from the bones, take care to keep the pieces of chicken in pleasing serving sizes. If this is not all eaten at the first serving, it makes a delicious casserole dish. It also freezes perfectly for a later serving.

Pork Chop Casserole

So easy to get ready and so pleasing to the eyes and taste buds!

4 medium-thick pork chops	Salt, pepper
6 tablespoons raw rice	1 can chicken broth
1 large onion	¼ teaspoon marjoram
2 ripe tomatoes	¼ teaspoon thyme
½ green pepper	

Brown pork chops in skillet; place chops on top of rice in fairly deep casserole and add pork chop drippings. Put a thick slice of onion and tomato, and a ring of pepper on top of each chop; salt and pepper each layer individually. Pour in broth and sprinkle with a couple of pinches each of marjoram and thyme. Bake at 350 degrees for one hour. Serves four. Make a double recipe and freeze one for a lazy day.

Spanish Steak Casserole

4 round steak servings	1 green pepper
6 tablespoons raw rice	Salt, pepper
2 large tomatoes	Dash of garlic salt
1 large onion	1 can chicken broth

Brown steak in salad oil. Place rice in bottom of casserole. Cut tomatoes into four slices, one for each steak; do the same with the onion. Place one slice of onion, pepper, and tomato on each steak, topping with the pepper rings. Salt and pepper each steak, add a dash of garlic salt.

Pour the chicken broth over this. Cover and bake at 350 degrees for one and one-half hours. Check for dryness after forty-five minutes. If dry, add more liquid. Water will be fine, but do not add too much.

Ginny's Pepper Steak with a Chinese Theme

Ginny cooks with a gourmet's flair. She calls this a "quick simple dinner for Sunday or patio."

1½ pounds flank steak	½ cup water
½ cup soy sauce	¼ cup salad oil
1 clove garlic	

Cut flank steak into diagonal paper thin slices, cutting with the grain of the meat. Combine soy sauce, garlic, and water; marinate meat in this for fifteen minutes. Heat oil in the skillet until very hot. Brown meat in oil quickly (about five minutes). Push meat to one side of pan and add the following:

2 medium-sized green peppers, thinly sliced	1 bunch celery, thinly sliced, diagonally
2 medium-sized onions, thinly sliced	1 rutabaga, thinly sliced, diagonally

Cook five minutes until vegetables are tender-crisp. Mix the remaining liquid with one tablespoon cornstarch and one-half cup water or one-half cup Sake if you have it. Sake is made from fermented rice. Stir into meat and vegetables and cook until thickened. Arrange on hot steamed rice, and garnish with tomato wedges. Serves four to six.

Note: If you cannot find a soy sauce that states on the label "Contents—soy," but instead says, "Hydrolized protein," do not make this without realizing that your dieter might be upset. If you wish to or need to substitute, try omitting the soy sauce. Instead, use Kitchen Bouquet, two teaspoons; one tablespoon molasses; and fill the one-half cup measure with water. In this case, thicken with soy flour rather than with the cornstarch. Season with one teaspoon salt.

Stuffed Veal Chops

With a sharp knife make a deep, wide slit in the fat side of a one and one-half inch thick veal chop. Fill each with two tablespoons of cranberry and orange relish. Close and sew up slits, or fasten by running skewers or toothpicks through edges. Dip chops in brown rice flour and brown in hot fat. Season with salt and pepper, add one-fourth cup water, cover, and bake at 300 degrees for about one hour. Check to see that it does not dry out. Serve with remaining relish, heated or raw. Allow one to a serving unless you have very hungry people.

Cranberry-Orange Relish

Grind one quart of cranberries and the rind of one large orange, mix with juice and one cup of sugar.

Elsie's English Spiced Meat

Elsie was Canadian-English and made this very delicious and unusual dish frequently during cold winter days in Vermont. Served hot, the pure meat juice makes gravy, served cold, with the meat pressed in a loaf pan, you will have a super jellied meat.

Purchase a lower leg of beef, about five pounds. (This has to be the part which has muscle to make the gelatin.)

Cut the leg into small chunks, put a layer of meat, salt, pepper, and six cloves into a bean pot. Layer meat in this manner up to the neck of the pot. Cover, wrap pot in several thicknesses of newspaper, and set into a kettle large enough to keep the bean pot half-covered with water during cooking period. *Cook about six hours. Do not put any water into the pot.*

Tuna Pie with Cheese Biscuit Crust

An old favorite revived.

3 tablespoon butter	½ teaspoon salt
½ cup sliced green pepper	3 cups milk
2 slices onion	1 large can tuna fish, drained
6 tablespoons rice flour	1 tablespoon lemon juice

Melt butter, add green pepper and onion, and cook until soft. Add flour and stir until well blended. Add salt, and add milk slowly, stirring constantly until thick and smooth. Bring to a boil, and boil two minutes. Add tuna and lemon juice. Pour into a quart baking dish, and cover with cheese rolls.

Cheese Biscuits

¾ cup milk	3 tablespoons butter
½ cup corn meal	¾ cup cheddar cheese, grated
1 cup rice flour	2 eggs
1 tablespoon baking powder	½ cup grated cheese
¾ teaspoon salt	2 canned pimientos
1 teaspoon potato flour	

Scald milk, add corn meal. Mix well and cool. Sift together twice the flour, baking powder, and salt (this includes the potato flour). Cut the butter into the flour mixture until it resembles fine bread crumbs. Add cheese and eggs to the milk-cornmeal mixture. Mix thoroughly. Turn out onto lightly floured board. Knead two to three minutes. Roll out one-half inch thick. Now, sprinkle with one-half cup grated cheese and two pimientos which have been cut fine. Roll up like a jelly roll, starting at the short side. With a sharp knife, cut into eight slices, flatten slightly, and place on top of creamed mixture in baking dish. Bake in hot oven at 450 degrees about thirty minutes, until browned. Serves eight. If you wish, you may add more tuna to the gravy.

Ham—Rice Timbales

3 cups cooked ground ham	½ teaspoon mustard (dry)
1 cup cooked rice	2 egg whites, slightly beaten
2 egg yolks, slightly beaten	
¼ cup mayonnaise	1 cup Rice Krinkles crumbs

Combine ham, rice, egg yolks, mayonnaise, and mustard, Shape into timbales. Dip in egg whites and roll in Rice Krinkle crumbs. Place each timbale on a slice of pineapple and bake at 350 degrees for twenty-five minutes.

Sauce

Make one and one-half cups medium cream sauce with rice flour as thickening; add one-half cup grated cheddar cheese and season to your taste. Pour several tablespoons over each baked timbale and sprinkle with paprika. Serves six people.

Crepes With an Italian Accent

You will be surprised how delicious a combination spinach, sausage, and cheese make!

3 eggs	2 teaspoons sugar
1¼ cups milk	4 teaspoons melted butter
1 cup brown rice flour	½ teaspoon salt
¼ cup rice polish	½ teaspoon baking powder

Beat eggs until light and frothy. Stir in salt, sugar, and butter. Sift flour with baking powder and add alternately with milk. Beat until smooth. Put a little salad oil into your skillet and tip skillet around quickly so pan is completely greased. Pour three to four tablespoons of batter into the pan and repeat turning so batter will run around pan thinly and completely cover the bottom. Turn heat down and let it cook through. The crepes need not be turned. Stack crepes in a towel until all are done. Spread each crepe with the filling, roll up, and arrange in shallow baking dish. Yield: twelve to fourteen crepes

Filling

Remove the casing from an uncooked five-ounce hot Italian sausage and saute the meat until golden brown;

break it up. Drain off all the fat and stir in one small clove garlic which has been pulverized. Cook one and one-half packages chopped frozen spinach according to package directions. Press out all liquid and add to the sausage alternating with one cup cooked chopped chicken, three-fourths cup grated Parmesan cheese, and a dash of onion salt.

Sauce

Melt six tablespoons of butter and blend in six table-spoons of rice flour until a smooth paste is formed. Add three cups of light cream; heat and stir until thickened. Add two cups grated Parmesan cheese, and one-half teaspoon onion juice. Heat and stir until cheese melts and flavors are blended.

Shrimp and Rice Bake

1 medium onion	½ teaspoon salt
1 small clove garlic	1½ cups cooked shrimp
¼ green pepper (medium size)	1 teaspoon oregano
2 tablespoons salad oil	1 cup cooked rice
1 can tomatoes (No. 2½ can)	½ cup grated sharp Cheddar cheese

Saute onion, garlic, and green pepper in oil; add tomatoes and bring to a boil. Simmer for fifteen minutes. Salt. Put cooked rice in casserole, toss shrimp and oregano with rice until blended; add tomato mixture and cheese, reserving enough cheese to sprinkle on top. Bake at 350 degrees for about thirty minutes. Serves four.

Crepes with Crab Meat

Another Sunday night supper dish—or for lunch. Follow recipe for French Pancakes. Keep crepes warm in oven between towels.

Season crab meat with salt and pepper to taste. One-half pound will serve approximately eight. Place crab meat in the center of the crepe and fold over twice. Place in

Pyrex casserole and cover with sauce given below; sprinkle tops with Swiss cheese, generously. Put under broiler until brown.

Sauce

2 tablespoons butter	1 tablespoon sherry wine
2 tablespoons rice flour	½ teaspoon salt
1 teaspoon onion juice	1 cup milk

Melt butter, add flour, and mix until smooth; slowly add onion juice, sherry, and milk, and cook until smooth and thickened.

Quickie

If you have French Pancake batter made up, follow their recipe for procedure. Keep crepes warm in the oven between towels. Season one can of tuna fish with whatever you may have on hand, such as a few pickles cut finely or ripe olives, a tablespoon of mayonnaise, salt, and pepper. Place the tuna in the center of the crepe, fold over once. Sprinkle top with grated cheese—Swiss or Cheddar or Mozarella, slip under broiler long enough to heat through and melt the cheese to the bubbly stage. Be sure to be generous with the cheese.

See how easy it can be? You may also use chicken or leftover ham in this manner.

Basic Quick Brown Rice

½ cup chopped scallions	½ teaspoon salt
½ cup chopped celery	1 cup Quick Brown Rice (I use MJB)
½ cup chopped green pepper	
½ cup butter or margarine	¼ teaspoon oregano
½ 6-ounce can of tomato paste	1 cup coarsely grated Cheddar cheese
2 cups water	

Saute scallions (you may use onion if you do not have the scallions), celery, and green pepper in butter until transparent. Mix tomato paste with a small amount of the water, and mix until thin enough to blend with other ingredients. Add remainder of the water, rice, oregano, and half of the cheese. Top with remaining cheese and bake for about thirty minutes at 350 degrees. Serves four generously.

Additions

Fold in one can of tuna, *or* fold in one-half pound ground beef which has been cooked until brown and done.

Rice Stuffing

Nice to use with turkey, chicken, or pork roast.

3 cups rice	¾ cup chopped celery leaves
6 cups water	1 tablespoon salt
¾ cup butter	¼ teaspoon each: pepper, sage
¾ cup chopped onion	and thyme
2 8-ounce cans mushrooms	¾ teaspoon marjoram
3 cups chopped celery	

Bring water to boil and add rice and one teaspoon salt. Reduce heat and cook for twenty to thirty minutes, or until rice is tender and fluffy. Saute onion, mushrooms, celery, and celery leaves in butter. Toss rice, seasonings, and all other ingredients lightly until thoroughly mixed. Spoon stuffing into a twelve to fifteen pound turkey, being careful not to pack. Or stuff two chickens or a crown roast of pork.

Harlene's Green Rice

Delicious, dependable, and different. Cook one cup of rice in two cups water with one teaspoon salt, then add two tablespoons butter. Bring to a boil, stir completely once. Lower heat and cook for about twenty minutes, or until the liquid has been absorbed and the rice is fluffy. Add the following:

1 egg, beaten	½ cup fresh parsley, ground
1 cup milk	or very finely chopped
1 medium onion, finely chopped	2 cups grated sharp Cheddar cheese

Reserve one-half cup of cheese to top the casserole. Blend all other ingredients with a tossing motion to avoid smashing rice kernels. Place in a quart casserole, sprinkle cheese over the top, sprinkle with paprika, and bake at 350 degrees for forty-five minutes. Serves six generously. If you wish to make this into a ring, pack into mold, place ring in pan of hot water, and bake forty-five minutes. Run spatula around mold and carefully invert it on a heated platter. The center may be filled with creamed shrimp or other seafood. If you choose the second procedure, you can serve eight.

I keep chicken broth on hand at all times. Be sure that it has nothing added to it other than salt. Since any bouillon or consomme that I have seen has ingredients forbidden to dieters, chicken broth fills the need in many recipes.

Rosemary Rice

1½ cups chicken broth	2 stalks celery
1 cup Quick Brown Rice	3 inches fresh rosemary
¼-½ cup butter	½ teaspoon salt
3 scallions (tops and all)	pepper

Bring chicken broth to boil, add rice and cook over low heat for fifteen minutes. Saute in butter scallions which have been finely cut with one-half inch chunks of celery and rosemary which has been stripped from the stem. Cook until transparent and tender, but with a tender-crispness to the celery. Remove from heat. When rice is done, toss celery-onion-rosemary mixture lightly with the rice and serve immediately. Serves four.

Green Pepper Boats

Fast and very filling. When a caller stayed too close to lunch time, my planned casserole turned into this quickie.

1 green pepper	2 slices of Jack cheese
1 can tuna fish	(Monterrey)
2 slices of Cheddar cheese	Paprika

Cut off the top of a green pepper, clean out the seeds; halve and cook in boiling water until tender, or about ten minutes. Fill half with tuna, top with slices of cheese—one slice of Jack and one slice of Cheddar; sprinkle with paprika and slide under broiler until the cheese melts and is slightly browned. Serve at once to two.

Ginny's Broiled Patio Sandwich

Serve on corn tortilla or brown rice waffle.

1 clove of garlic (mashed)	1 small can chopped black olives
1 tablespoon oil	
10 ounces Cheddar cheese	1 8-ounce can tomato sauce

If using tortilla, brush with oil or butter and slide under the broiler until brown and crisp. If using a waffle, bake and have ready. Soak garlic in oil while making the other preparations. Grate the cheese; mix all of the ingredients together and blend well. Spread generously over tortilla or waffle and broil for four to five minutes, or until brown. Serves six.

Scalloped Potatoes

When you live on a diet which excludes almost all of the quick dishes which most people take for granted from their grocery stores, every quick dish is important. This way of fixing potatoes is delicious, easy, and so quick that by the time your table is set, salad made, meat sliced, and family called to dinner, the potatoes will be done. This recipe serves three people generously.

2 medium potatoes	1 large scallion, top and all
½ cup butter or margarine (⅛ pound)	Salt, pepper, and savory
	Milk

Slice potatoes as thin as you can easily. If they are young potatoes with good skins, scrub and leave skin on. The skins add so much flavor as well as nutritional value. Melt butter in heavy frying pan with a tight cover. Slice scallion, top and all, into butter, add enough potatoes to cover bottom of pan, and brown slightly, turning a few times. Add the rest of the potatoes, pour enough milk over them to have the milk show around the potatoes, but not enough to cover them. Sprinkle with salt, hand-ground pepper if you have it, and savory; cover pan tightly, turn heat low and cook until tender. This will take fifteen to twenty minutes.

Cheese Whiz

A real quickie in preparation time.
Preheat oven to 350 degrees

4 sections of baked waffle	1 cup milk
4 slices of Cheddar cheese	¼ teaspoon salt
2 eggs	Pepper and cayenne pepper

Place the waffle sections in a shallow greased baking dish. Place one slice of Cheddar cheese on each section; beat the eggs with the milk, add the salt, pour over the waffles and sprinkle with cayenne very lightly and more liberally with black pepper. Bake for one hour. If you wish, garnish with strips of crisp bacon. Serves two generously.

Hot Cheese Tart

Wonderful for lunch with a crisp salad! Somewhat like a custard with a crisp crust to contrast. A good mixture to pour over waffle squares and bake also.

¾ pound Swiss cheese, grated	¼ teaspoon basil
3 eggs	1 teaspoon salt
1¾ cups milk	Dash of cayenne pepper
2 tablespoons minced onion	Dash of black pepper
¼ teaspoon oregano	Parmesan cheese

Beat three eggs until light. Add cheese, milk, onion, and seasonings. Pour into a 9-inch pie plate which has been lined with pastry. Sprinkle with Parmesan cheese, about one-fourth cup, or as you wish. Bake at 450 degrees for fifteen minutes. Reduce heat to 300 degrees and bake until set, about thirty minutes. Cut into wedges and serve to six or eight, depending upon your appetites.

Corn Bread and Sausage Stuffing

For a ten to twelve-pound turkey.

Make a double recipe of Corn Muffins found on Page 28. Bake and break into fairly fine crumbs. Place in shallow pan in a 300 degree oven, stirring occasionally until crumbs are dried out. If you like a moist dressing, you may skip this step.

1¼ cups finely chopped onion	1 tablespoon salt
1 pound small link sausages	1½ teaspoons black pepper
½ cup butter or margarine	1½ teaspoons thyme
1 cup finely chopped celery	6 to 8 cups corn bread crumbs
½ cup chopped celery tops	¾ cup water or wine
(the fine leaves)	

Saute the sausages in the melted butter with the onion and celery and celery tops. Add the salt, pepper, and thyme to the bread crumbs, mixing thoroughly; add to the sausage mixture, then add the liquid. Stuff the turkey. If you wish, substitute your favorite ingredient for the sausage, such as bacon, oysters, or water chestnuts. In this case, you may wish to adjust the seasoning slightly to compensate for the highly-seasoned sausage. Be sure and always check sausage content to be certain that the enemy is not present.

Section 9

HAVING THE "LAST WORD"

As I put the final touches on this little cookbook, my thoughts push ahead to so many experiments yet untried. But I do have to stop somewhere, I tell myself. Actually, these recipes are only the launching pad for many, many more, and I hope that all who use them will make them just that. Favorite recipes using wheat can be adapted into rice almost without exception; yeast recipes will not work.

In my small area of contact, I have been able to help people with grain allergies. It is my prayer that this book will lift wheat-free diets out of eating for survival into delightful eating.

Section 10

TABLE OF COMPARISON OF FOOD VALUES
OF WHEAT–RICE–SOY

Eating products made from rice, corn, soya, and potato flours, rather than wheat, rye, barley, and oats flours, promotes questions regarding the nutritional values of the new grains.

In Table I given below, I have included only those categories which are most frequently mentioned in the buying and cooking experiences of the average housewife. Since rice, supplemented by soya flour, is the basis of this cookbook, I have attempted to show what happens to the food values when this substitution for wheat is made. You will note that I have presented this information *on the flours with the exception of the whole brown rice grain and the white rice grain.* I was unable to find a flour breakdown on them.

I wrote to Mrs. Dorothy Hutcheson, Institutional and Consumer Director, Home Economics Department, Rice Council, Houston, Texas, for help with the above problem. She replied, "In our research, we have found rice flour to have the same composition as rice. One pound of white rice flour equals one pound of regular milled white rice in composition. The same applies to other types of rice."

If the reader wishes to follow through with a few mathematical problems—it is very gratifying to figure the nutrient value of 200 grams of whole wheat opposed to a mix of 100 grams of natural brown rice flour plus 50 grams of rice polish and 50 grams of soya flour. This is the ratio I use in the waffle recipe I use most frequently. Under this combination, protein, calcium, and vitamin B (namely thiamine,

103

TABLE I

COMPARISON OF FOOD VALUES–WHEAT–RICE–SOY*

| 100 Grams Edible Portion | | 1 Ounce Equals 31.10 Grams | | | | | 1 Cup Equals 8 Ounces | |
Food and Description	Food Energy Calories	Protein Grams	Calcium Milligrams	Iron Milligrams	Thiamine Milligrams	Riboflavin Milligrams	Niacin Milligrams
Whole Wheat Flour	333	13.3	41	3.3	.55	.12	4.3
Brown Rice (whole)	360	7.5	32	1.6	.34	.05	4.7
White Rice (whole) unenriched	363	6.7	24	.8	.07	.03	1.6
White Rice (whole) enriched	363	6.7	24	2.9	.44	**	3.5
Soy Bean (full fat flour)	421	36.7	199	8.4	.85	.31	2.1
Rice Polish	265	12.1	69	16.1	1.84	.18	28.2
Rice Bran	276	13.3	76	19.4	2.26	.25	29.8

*The information in this table was taken from the *Composition of Foods*, Agricultural Handbook No. 8, Agricultural Research Service, U.S.D.A. (Revised December, 1963).

**Minimum and maximum requirements for riboflavin have not been specified as yet by the U.S. Government.

riboflavin, and niacin) take a tremendous leap in our dieters favor. In addition, this makes a very good combination flavorwise.

REFERENCES

1. Treatment malabsorption syndrome. *Mod. Treat.* Hoeber Medical Division, March, 1965. Report of Studies of Dicke, W. K.: *Celiac Disease;* H. A. Weijers, M. D., and J. H. van deKamer, Ph.D.

2. *Composition of Foods, Agriculture Handbook No. 8.,* Agricultural Research Service, United States Department of Agriculture.

3. *America's Cookbook,* New York Herald Tribune Home Institute.

4. *Batters and Doughs,* University of Arizona, Tucson, Arizona.

5. *Gluten-Free Diet,* The Clinical Center, Nutrition Department, National Institutes of Health, Bethesda, Maryland.

6. "Diagnosis and Therapy." *Merck's Manual,* Merck, Sharp, and Dohme Research Laboratory, 1961.

7. Patient's diet supplied by Dr. William E. Bishop, Globe, Arizona.

GLOSSARY

Brown Rice Flour

This is the whole unpolished grain of rice, ground into flour. Only the outer hull and a small amount of bran have been removed. Thus the remaining bran and all of the polish (inner bran layers and the rice germ) remain in the flour.

Rice Bran

Rice bran is a soft fluffy product obtained from polishing the natural brown rice kernel into the white rice kernel. These outer bran layers contain a high concentration of minerals (iron, calcium, phosphorus, and potassium) and the vitamin B family, also vitamin E. Rice bran also rates very high in protein. It is often used as a booster of nutrients just as the wheat world uses wheat germ.

Rice Polish

This is the inner bran layers made into flour. It is a by-product from polishing natural brown rice into white rice. It, too, contains a high concentration of minerals and vitamins. It is creamy white in color, as opposed to the tan color of the bran. It is also added to foods for a nutrient boost.

White Rice Flour

This is the polished white rice reduced to flour. It can be used interchangeably with the natural brown rice flour. If you will study the nutrient table on Page 104, you will note that unless the flour is enriched, its values are much less. I very rarely use it, as I found it more granular upon the tongue. My reaction continues to be why use it when the brown rice flour offers so much more in texture, taste, and food value?

Soya Flour

This flour is recommended by the mills for use in home cooking as opposed to *soy flour*. It has been lightly toasted to aid assimilation and is designed to preserve full nutritional value, according to the mills' description of it. Soya flour imparts a hint of nuts and slightly sweet flavor to products in which it is used; it also imparts smoothness and richness. It is very good in cookies. Because of its heaviness, it is generally used in a ratio of not more than one-quarter soya flour to three-quarters other flour. In many waffle recipes, I use one-half cup soya, one-half cup rice polish or rice bran, and one cup of natural brown rice flour.

Potato Flour

Potato flour is starch. Actually, it is the whole potato, steam-cooked and dried. One pound of potato flour is said to be equal to five pounds of potatoes. It *must* be thoroughly blended with other dry ingredients before mixing into dough or else lumps appear and spoil the dough or batter. It may be creamed with the shortening. It provides "togetherness" in doughs and batters and improves the texture. It is an excellent thickener. It is best used in small amounts with other flour.

Carob

This is also called St. John's Bread. It may be used as a substitute for chocolate. It tastes much like chocolate and is said not to irritate those who are allergic to chocolate. It comes in a powder like cocoa, a drink mix, and a bar like chocolate.

INDEX

ALLERGIES, ix, 4, 6, 102

BASIC FLOUR, xi, 7
Best Recipe, xiv
BREAD, 13-36
  apricot, 22
  best bread, 17
  Boston brown, 21
  cheese corn meal biscuits, 23
  cheese daisies, 31
  cheese surprise, 31
  cheese torte, 30
  corn loaf, 18
  corn sticks, 24
  crisp corn pone, 19
  flour medley, 19
  Hila's garlic grits, 20
  orange-date, 16
  plain brown rice, 17
  popovers, 29
  prune, 21
  rice bran, 15-16
  rice sesame seed I, II, 14-15
  Sara's noodles, 36
  Sesame seed crackers I, II, 23
  spoon, 19, 20
Muffins, 26-29
  blueberry, 27
  bran, 28
  corn, 28
  corn-potato, 26
  flour medley, 29
  molasses-bran, 29
  tea, 27
Pancakes, basic recipe, 32
  blueberry, 32
  cheese blintze, 35
  corn meal and rice, 33
  French pancakes or crepes, 34
    sauce for, 34
  hominy, 33
  orange, 35
  rice bran, 33
Waffles, 24-26
  basic recipe, 24
  combination, 25
  corn flour, 26

  corn meal, 25
  ginger bread, 26
  rice polish, 25
BREAD, problems of making, 13-14
  without gluten, 13-14
BRONCHIECTASIS, 4
Brown Rice Flour, 109

Carob, as a substitute for
  chocolate, 38, 40
  definition, 110
CELIAC DISEASE, 3
Chinese dishes
  pitfalls, 9
Chocolate
  substitute for, 38
Cocktail
  forbidden grain content, 9
Coffee, instant, 9, 10
CAKES, 37-48
  problems in making without
    gluten, 37, 38
  cheese cake, 48
  chocolate or cocoa roll, 40
  chocolate log, 44
    frosting for, 44
  Dorothy's applesauce cake, 46
    frosting for, 46
  Dutch Cream cake topping, 42
  Fudge cake, 43
    frosting for, 43
  German chocolate cake and frost-
    ing, 46-48
  lemon filling for cake, 41
  Marian's whipped cream frost-
    ing, 42
  orange spongecake, 39
  peppermint rum fluff filling,
    44-45
  prune cake, 45, 46
  sponge cake, 42
  sponge jelly roll, 40
  zabaglione cake, 38
COOKIES, 49-59
  Abbie's hermit cookies, 57
  apricot, 57
  basic cookie recipe, 52

cherry buttons, 53
chocolate chip, 51
chocolate chip and coconut, 53
coconut macaroons, 56
date balls, 54
fig or date bars, 56
fruit balls, 49
fruit bar cookies, 55
fruit cookies, 49
German chocolate brownies, 50
ginger date, 54
Ida's sesame seed, 50
layer date bars, 55
    filling for, 55
meringues, 58

DESSERTS, 60-73
caramel syrup for, 73
Carol's fudge sauce for, 73-74
chocolate mint roll, 63
chocolate surprise, 61-62
chocolate syrup for, 73
Clara's lemon chiffon pudding,
    66
cranberry frappe, 61
cream puffs, eclairs or fritters,
    70-73
    cream filling for, 72-73
    quick and easy filling for
        cream puffs, 72
    croquembouche, and mold
        for, 71
date tarts, 67
Dorothy's marshmallow crunch
    cups, 67
eclairs, 72
fluffy fig pudding, 67-68
French custard, 64
French pastry cream, 71
fritters, 72
frozen lemon cream, 61
grasshopper, 69
hot fruit medley, 65
lemon chiffon ring with
    fresh fruit, 65-66
lemon sherbet, 60
Mary Ellen's ice cream, 60
party glamour, 68
peppermint cream filling for
    cream puffs, 70
peppermint ice cream, 62
petite puffs, 72

pink velvet, 68
refrigerator mint ice cream, 63
tangerine-yogurt sherbet, 60-61
DICKE, W. K., 3
DIET,
    REASONS FOR, vii-ix, 3-7
    wheat, rye, barley, oats: elimi-
        nation of, 3-7
DIET research by:
    W. K. Dicke, H. A. Weijers, J. H.
        van de Kamer, 3

Eggs, as a binder, 37-38
    in relation to lightness and tex-
        ture, 37

Flour adjustments, 6
FRIEND AND FOE, 8-12
    hidden parts of grains, 8-12
    list of, 10-12
    sections:
        beverages, 10
        cereals, 11
        crackers and substitutes, 11
        dairy products, 10, 11
        desserts, 10
        meat, fish, poultry, 11-12
        meat tenderizer, 12
        miscellaneous, 12
        monosodium glutamate, 12
        sauces, 12
        soups, 11
        thickening ingredients, 10

GASTRO-INTESTINAL UPSETS
    linked to wheat, 4
Gelatin, use of, 13
Gliadin, 3
GLOSSARY, 109
GLUTEN, viii, ix, 3-7
    effect of elimination, 5, 7
    its effect on baked products, 3, 4,
        6
Gluten-enteropathy, viii

Health of Modern Man
    avenues for improvement, vii
Hidden Ingredients
    wheat or gluten-gliaden grains,
        8-12

IDIOPATHIC STEATORRHEA, 3
Ingredients, label check, 9-12

LABELS, IMPORTANCE OF, 9-12
Leavening, 13, 37, 38

MAIN DISHES, 84-101
  apple-stuffed pork chops, 87
  basic quick brown rice, 96-97
  Carol's Seafood Newberg, 86
  cheese rolls, 93
  cheese whiz, 100
  chicken avocado supreme, 89
  chicken rosemary, 88
  corn bread and sausage stuffing,
    101
  crepes with crab meat, 95-96
  crepes with an Italian accent,
    94
  Elsie's English spiced meat, 92
  Ginny's broiled patio sandwich,
    99
  Ginny's pepper steak, 91
  green pepper boats, 98-99
  ham-rice timbales, 94
  Harlene's green rice, 97-98
  hot cheese tart, 100-101
  Marian's rolled rump roast, 86-87
  oyster rarebit, 84-85
  pimiento rice, 89-90
  pork chop casserole, 90
  quickie, 96
  rice stuffing, 97
  rosemary rice, 98
  scalloped oysters, 84
  scalloped potatoes, 99-100
  seafood casserole, 85-86
  shrimp and rice bake, 95
  Spanish steak casserole, 90
  stuffed veal chops, 92
    cranberry-orange relish for, 92
  Syrian lamb stew, 87-88
  tuna pie with cheese roll crust,
    93
MALABSORPTION SYNDROME,
  vii, 3
Malt, definition of, 8
Mexican food at restaurants,
  pitfalls, 9
Mix, make your own, 14
  muffins, 27-29

NON-TROPICAL SPRUE, 3
Nutritional value of grains, 103

Pancakes, 31-35
PASTRY, 76

Pastry and Pies, 75-83
  problems in making, 75
  chocolate coconut pie shell, 77
  coconut pie shell, 77
  cream cheese crust, 76
  Creme de Menthe pie, 77
  frozen eggnog pie and filling, 79
  Grandmother's pumpkin pie, 82
  Jane's cherry cream pie, 80
  Krinkle crunch pie, 81-82
  lemon chiffon pie, 78-79
  lemon meringue pie, 83
  mocha chiffon, 81
  peppermint chiffon pie, 82
  Rice Krinkle crust, 77
  Sue's meringue, 83
  super rhubarb cream pie, 78
Potato Flour
  definition and use, 110
  to improve texture and
    togetherness, 13, 38

Rice Bran, 109
Rice Flour, see Glossary, 109
  as a basic flour, xi, 7
  nutrient content, 104
  ratio in use—to other flour,
    see pancakes, 32, 103
  wheat substitute, 103
Rice Polish, see Glossary, 109

Soups, 9, 11
Soya Flour, see Glossary, 110
  nutrient table, 104
St. John's Bread, see Carob, 110
  definition and use, 38, 110

TABLE   OF   COMPARISON   OF
  FOOD VALUES, 103
Texture,
  ways to achieve, 13, 37, 38

van deKamer, J. H., 3

Waffles, 24-26
Weijers, H. A., 3
WHEAT
  compensation for its baking
    qualities, 3-4, 6, 7
  content of, 3
  compensation for its
    elimination, 13, 37, 38
White Rice Flour, 109

Yeast, bakers, 13
Yeast bread, 6
Yeast, brewers
    definition, 8